Real Crime Forensic Files

RACHEL HUDSON

DEDICATION

In the memory of a best friend, Joseph Evans.

CONTENTS

ACKNOWLEDGMENTS

I want to thank everyone who has helped me to write this book.

1 THE SEARCH FOR LISA RENE

A teenage immigrant came to the United States to realize her dream of becoming a doctor, but a tragic twist of fate intervened. When she found herself an innocent victim of the drug trade kidnap. Jen held captive. She survived for days against all odds. The authorities arrested her captors, but they refuse to reveal her whereabouts, the FBI and local police raced against time determined to save the teenager's life.

When a young woman was grabbed from a Texas home, the police raced to find her abductors on the face of it. The kidnapping seemed like the random act of desperate men. Before the FBI could find her, they first had to find a motive. Their investigation revealed a complex story of betrayal and revenge at its center stood an innocent 16 year old who found herself in the clutches of killers.

On September 24th, 1994, Arlington, Texas, it was a Saturday night and 16 year old, Lisa Renee was home studying. She wanted to make the most of her first semester in an American high school, she hoped to someday return to the Virgin Islands.

As a surgeon, her concentration was suddenly shattered. Somehow. She knew not to answer the door. Instead, she called her sister.

Pearl told Lisa to call 911. She promised to come right home.

Arlington 911. What are you reporting?

What do they say that they're looking for men we're trying to break into her house? Claim to be FBI agents.

The dispatcher heard the phone.

Then there was shyness. Lisa never came back on the line.

As Arlington, Texas police responded to the 911, Lisa disappeared into the night.

The police had no way of knowing they were about to pass her on the street. Or that a 16 year old girl was now in mortal danger.

Police were on the scene with Lisa's sister Pearl.

When detective John Stanton arrived as a veteran of the Arlington police force, he would lead the investigation.

From the initial 911 call, it sounded like a very serious kidnapping. Uh, it sounded to the nine 11 call takers, uh, that there was some foul play and some actual violence involved. The detective needed to know everything and quickly the early hours of a kidnapping case, a crucial girl told the officers all she knew.

She was at work when her sister Lisa called to say, some men were trying to break into the apartment. She told Lisa to call 911, then hurried home.

But she was too late. She found the sliding glass door smashed, and Lisa gone for a 16 year old to be physically dragged from. Uh, residence, um, in Arlington is just, it's really kind of unspeakable. Where was it? Hurl told the detectives that her brothers, Neil and Stanfield were also staying with her. They had been evicted from their own apartment for allegedly selling drugs.

Pearl explained that her family was from the US Virgin Islands. She ended up brothers had come to America first. Lisa had joined them in time to start school. She was a straight, a student investigators process, the apartment, hoping to find a clue as to the abductors identities. They found no prints foreign to the apartment.

Perhaps the abductors were known to the family. The detective asked to talk to Pearl's brothers that they were on their way back from a Houston music festival. The detective told Pearl to get them on the phone.

They were 50 miles from the apartment when detective Stanton reached them. When I spoke to the brothers, I spoke with Stanfield. Initially Stanfield told me that. They don't know of anyone who would have wanted to UB their sister. They owed no one money, uh, that this was not about any sort of drug business.

They weren't involved in anything involving drugs. As much as Pearl Rene tried to help the detective believed her brothers had the answers he was looking for.

But without their help, he would have to identify leases, captures the hard way as precious minutes, slipped by forensic technicians, combed the apartment for additional clues. They collected glass from the broken sliding door and hair and fiber samples. Awesome. For fingerprints only to conclude that the kidnappers had worn gloves, even this small detail, we're a detectives.

It suggested Lisa Rene was in the hands of experienced criminals. If detective Stanton ever hoped to find Lisa alive, he knew he needed all the help. He could get, you have to use the resources available to you. And that includes additional manpower. Uh, the use of the FBI. You have to use everything that you have as a resource.

Special agents from the FBI's Fort Worth resident agency joined detectives at the scene. Special agent. Kenneth persona was concerned that the kidnappers had identified themselves as FBI agents, as it turned out, there was no FBI agent there on the scene or any other joint investigation ongoing in that neighborhood.

Neighbors reported seeing four young African-American men hanging around the apartment complex prior to the abduction, they were wearing camouflage clothing and driving a champagne colored Cadillac. The atmosphere at the crime scene was tense. Um, Lisa Renee's sister was very distraught that she wasn't there for her sister and also.

Residents in the complex, uh, were disturbed that a young lady could be abducted from an apartment complex. So readily the fact that Lisa Rene was a minor and that her abductors and impersonated, federal agents gave the FBI jurisdiction over the case, they would work in conjunction local laws.

Homicide detective Stanton worked through the night and into the morning in the early hours of September 25th, he received a call from Lisa's brothers. They had found the champagne colored Cadillac in nearby Irving. The same one residents had described at the complex. It wasn't unusual tip for the brothers to have just barely gotten into Arlington.

To have had them drive mysteriously to a residence in Irving, Texas, which is some distance from Arlington. And in that same bit of circumstance find a Cadillac fitting that general description. We thought it was very curious. They reported that the Cadillac was parked in front of a residence. If Lisa's brothers knew something more about their sister's abduction, they weren't telling police

Detective Stanton and special agent persona rushed to the residence in Irving Irving police were already there.

As soon as they found out where Lisa was being held, the better their chance of finding her alive as Lisa's brothers had said. The Cadillac was parked out front. I had a cold hood. We touched the vehicle to see if the vehicle had been moved or had been in operation previously from a heat on the hood. We also looked inside the vehicle with our flashlights to see if there were any items, uh, that may have been left by the victim.

The woman answered the door.

We explained. Why we were there, that we were from their Arlington police department, from the FBI. We'd like to talk to her about the abduction of a young 16 year old girl. We asked if we may just look around her home to see if the young lady that was abducted was in there. The woman said she and her husband owned the Cadillac, but he wasn't home.

Since he worked the night shift.

She said she hadn't seen anyone who matched the description of the suspect. But she let investigators take a quick look around.

They began in the child's room where her son was asleep. Nothing seemed suspicious.

In another room, they awakened a woman sleeping in a double bed. It appeared she was alone. Sandra. She tells me we look around, we're looking for somebody to just sit tight in the hallway. Investigators noticed stairs to an attic.

One of the Irving officers climbed up and looked around here.

He checked amidst the boxes and other items, but saw no one there. We didn't have a real just cause too. Do an intensive search of the residence. Um, we searched for obviously any sign that someone had been kidnapped in places where someone could secrete a human body, uh, just to be on the safe side.

Investigate is left still suspicious, but without a warrant, they were unable to do a more thorough search.

Investigators turned their attention back to Lisa's brother, Neil and Stanfield. We felt that it was drug-related and we told Neil and Stanford that we're not interested. Uh, in their current legal problems, but that we feel like Lisa's life may be at stake and that we need to have all the information that they can provide us, uh, to help get their sister back the day after the kidnapping investigators, again, interviewed Neil and Stanfield.

Despite their pending drug charges. Lisa's brothers finally came clean. They described a bogus drug deal that they'd taken part in a few days before the brothers said that they had met with two men, but claimed the only knew the one named Steve now, Steve and his partner had given them $5,000 to score nine pounds of marijuana. Hello, Neil and Stanfield promised they would return in an hour with the drugs. But they never made it right. They now admit it.

They had never intended to deliver the marijuana. They just needed the money for attorney's fees because of their pending drug charges.

Lisa's brothers said they didn't know how to contact Steve, but they knew someone who did. And that was all the brothers would say.

The man who knew it was an inmate serving an eight year sentence at the Tarrant County jail.

He revealed that Steve's full name was Stephen Beckley, a 19 year old who worked detailing cars at a dealership in Irving, Texas. There investigators ran a computer check on Beckley. He had no outstanding warrants and no criminal history. As investigators continued to work the case Lisa's sister Pearl did all she could to help.

She hung up missing persons, flyers and contacted local media, hoping someone might've seen Lisa, but the chance of finding her sister alive grew dimmer with each passing day.

On September 24th, 1994, she was kidnapped from her Arlington, Texas apartment. Oh, who are you? Oh,

BI ma'am.

Just over two days in past, since Lisa's desperate call for help, local police and the FBI were no closer to finding the missing girl with time running out, the Arlington police department asked the public for help. Detective Stanton recalls. The response was tremendous. It was truly, uh, something that brought out, uh, the public and the public's fears about being abducted out of your own residence.

It's sort of something that you're not expecting, um, in a community like Arlington, it's not something that's ordinary. Uh, this doesn't happen here. Um, I would say ever in a town that like ours on September 27th, the Arlington police detective received an unexpected visitor. He was the owner of the Irving, Texas home that police had searched in connection with a champagne colored Cadillac.

He was at work during the search, but had since heard the news of Lisa's disappearance and believed he had information that might be helpful. You know, these people. But he said that the day before the kidnapped, he threw a barbecue. Since his wife's brothers were staying with them for a few days.

The oldest brother, Orlando hall was involved with drugs.

His younger brother, Demetrius hall shared the same interest. They're friends, Steven Beckley joined them. When the husband told us that the hall brothers were dressed in camouflage clothing, it made him know that after having heard the news stories, his brothers in law could very well be connected to the kidnapping case.

Um, the night something else had sparked the man suspicions of the neighbors said she saw several young men drive up to the house in his Cadillac. At that time, he and his wife were out for dinner using a different car, but the Cadillac's keys were kept in the hall. So it was possible. His wife's brothers had borrowed it.

The man said he'd never trusted. The whole brothers, both had served time in Arkansas on drug charges. And by visiting their sister in Irving, Texas, they were in violation of their parole hearing. Whatever the man, since they were up to something new, but didn't know

He added that the hall brothers were no longer staying at his house whatsoever. On the night of the kidnapping. Only Orlando had slept in the house, but he flew back to Arkansas early, the next morning, planning to stay with friends in the town of Eldoret. Nobody, since the barbecue detective suspected, Orlando had probably joined the others there.

Yeah, he contacted the Eldorado Arkansas police investigators discovered that 19 year old Demetrius hall was on parole for possession of cocaine. With intent to distribute. His older brother, Orlando hall was on parole for the same offense. His record also included arrests for aggravated assault and carrying a weapon.

When I spoke to the people in Eldorado, they were aware of the hall family. And in fact, they were providing to me information about the hall brothers before I could even give them the information about the hall brothers. Uh, they were well known to law enforcement in the community. Later that day, investigators obtained a warrant to more thoroughly search the urban Texas home, where the hall brothers have been staying.

Scoured the house for hair fibers, blood fingerprints, and anything else that might be connected to the crime

FBI, special agent Garrett, Floyd remembers their most significant decision in the children's room. We found. And souvenir miniature baseball bat. When you pick up an item and you can see glass embedded in it, and you know, the sliding pane window was glass. Then you make a decision on the spot and you believe that evidence is a part of the crime scene.

Lab tests would determine whether his hunch was correct.

In a storage container found in a bedroom closet. Investigators discovered a green knit shirt with insulation fibers on it.

They bagged it for further analysis.

They also took samples of insulation fibers from the attic. Lab tests would later reveal that they matched the fibers on the shirt.

A pair of camouflage pants was also found in the attic.

Forensic technicians processed the champagne colored Cadillac at the police impound. Lot.

They found no fingerprints relevant to the case. They did discover a few small blast fragments inside the car, possibly from Lisa's sliding glass door. They sent the fragments to the lab for analysis.

As they waited for the results agents obtained arrest warrants for the hall brothers and their friend, Steven Beckley, since they already had enough to establish probable cause, but they still hadn't found Lisa Rene. Agent Floyd continued to work around the clock, knowing that with each hour, they were less likely to find her alive.

We're very motivated in solving this case. And as much as we knew that time was critical, all of our efforts were focus on the recovery of the victim. Investigators, hope they could pick up Lisa's trail, a trail that ended with broken glass. Technicians compared glass fragments from the car and those embedded in the baseball bat to shards collected from Lisa's home at the FBI laboratory in Washington, DC supervisory, special agent and forensic examiner. Bruce Hall attempted to confirm that all the glass had come from the same sliding glass door.

Technicians examined the glass embedded in the baseball. Wow.

They tested the composition of the glass. It was consistent with the glass collected, at least as a partner to confirm their results. They also tested its refractive index. The degree to which light bends as it passes through the sample. After characterizing the glass recovery from the crime scene and characterizing the glass recovered from the baseball bat.

I found that the glass on the baseball bat had the same refractive index and same composition as the glass at the crime scene. That led me to the conclusion that the glass on the baseball bat had originated from the crime scene. The glass found in the Cadillac did not match. It was determined to have come from a window previously broken on the car.

The request of the FBI and Arlington, Texas police Eldorado, Arkansas detectives tracked down the fugitives.

They found 19 year old Demetrius hole at his father's house and elderly credo.

He surrendered peacefully and it was taken to the Eldorado jail. Yeah.

But he refused to say anything about Lisa's whereabouts the search of the house revealed nothing. What investigators still didn't know? Was where Lisa was and whether she was dead or alive?

Four and a half, two days after 16 year old, Lisa remains kidnapped from her sister's apartment in Arlington, Texas investigators to Eldorado Arkansas.

One of the three suspects Demetrius hall was in custody. Investigators continued to search for his older brother, Orlando. And a third man named Steven Becky.

That afternoon police found Stephen Beckley at a friend's house. The officers didn't even have to knock Beckley, came out and gave himself up.

Yeah. Agents and detectives from Arlington flew to Eldorado to interview the suspects.

Steven Beckley was initially uncooperative. He refused to say where Elisa Renee was or whether she was still alive. Special agent Garrett, Floyd refused to give up Mr. Beckley advised that he did not know a whole lot of information concerning what was going on after about an hour of talking to him. He looked at me and we developed somewhat of a relationship and we started to talk.

Beckley said that he and his friends had called in a fourth man named Bruce Webster to help them exactly revenge on Lisa Renee's brothers.

Webster was a convicted felon and had a violent reputation as a Hitman. Their plan was to dowse Lisa Renee's brothers and gasoline, and ignite it. If they didn't turn over the drugs or the money as they had promised.

When the men arrived at Lisa Rene's apartment, her brothers were not home unwilling to leave. They kidnapped her and instead. Beckley said that he and the other three took Lisa to the house in Irving, Texas, where Demetrius and Orlando were staying at.

He transferred the teenage girl from the Cadillac to Becky's Ford escort. Get off the clock. Then Beckley Bruce Webster and 19 year old Demetrius hall drove her to Arkansas. Orlando hall stayed behind and hid in his sister's attic. Detective Stanton was frustrated. Police had been within a few feet of Orlando hall and missed him.

It wasn't until later that we learned, uh, after we had taken some people into custody that Orlando had been indeed hiding in the attic insulation. While we were downstairs, uh, talking to the lady of the house. Beckley said that during the four hour drive to Arkansas, he and the other two had taken turns raping Lisa Rene.

When they arrived in Arkansas Webster booked a motel Roman pine bluff, Lisa was kept bound and gagged and went bathroom. Yeah, I'm trying to find agents pushed Beckley to tell them if the girl was still alive and where she was every minute counted. If they were to save her life. But Begley wouldn't say he claimed he was afraid to talk.

As long as Bruce Webster was on the loose. In his mind, he thought believed, knew that Bruce Webster would kill him or anyone else. If they ever divulged information on what it occurred to Lisa Rene, that's the fear that Bruce Webster had instilled in the individuals as part of his kidnapping. If I say a word Beckley did tell investigators where to look for Webster.

The ex-convict might still be at the motel in Pine Bluff, where they had held Lisa Rene four days ago.

Investigators headed to the motel to confront a man Beckley had described as a violent Hitman

Pine Bluff was 90 miles from elder radar agent spoke with a manager to confirm Beckley story. They hope they would find Webster there as well as Lisa Rene, upon interviewing the innkeeper, we were able to determine that Bruce Webster had registered at that end. And at, during the time he was registering a young lady attempted to get out of the car and that Bruce turned to the other occupants in the car and says, put the bitch back in the car.

Bruce Webster and his companions then drove to the back of the property and went into the room. The manager also remembered seeing two other black males in the car, but she couldn't make out their faces. She showed investigators the registration log for September 25th, Webster had been in room five 13.

The room was rented and cleaned several times after the men checked out, chances of finding any useful evidence were slim.

An FBI emergency response team was called in the agent and detective continued to interview Beckley. They asked him for details of what went on in the room, hoping he would break down and tell them where Lisa was now. Once we got Mr. Beckley to this Pine Bluff motel. The urgency was there in that we thought that she was still alive because Mr.

Beckley assured us the last time he saw her, she was alive and she was at this end. Okay. Beckley told police that the men had raped Lisa repeatedly in the bathroom. Otherwise they'd kept her hooded. It was a paper bag over her head during their second night at the motel, the kidnappers were nearly discovered a security guard knocked at the door,

Complaining or ask that they're on residents, security guard who live there. Check the room to see if everything was all right. The security guard did check the room and did not see Lisa Rene within the room. Steven Beckley advise that had he seen her, that they were going to kill security. Exactly. And the others were afraid that the guard might return.

The motel was no longer a safe place to hide.

As the kidnapper told his story, forensic technicians work to confirm that Lisa had in fact been in the room, but after hours of painstaking work, they still had no evidence that Lisa had been there or that she was still alive.

Six days after 16 year old, Lisa Rene was kidnapped from her Arlington, Texas apartment. The FBI was no closer to finding her or two remaining suspects. Although investigators had found no evidence to indicate that Lisa had been in a Pine Bluff motel confessed kidnapper, Steven Beckley assured them. She had.

Forensic technician. Joel Stevenson of the Arlington Texas police department was determined to find something that would corroborate Beckley story. We went in knowing that possibly sexual assaults had occurred in that motel room, multiple sexual assaults. Uh, we went into the motel room looking for body fluids, uh that may tie the suspects to the motel room or Lisa to the motel room.

If Lisa and her kidnappers had left behind any evidence, it appeared to have been destroyed by the motels housekeepers. The technicians didn't give up. They continued their meticulous search for hairs, fibers, and fingerprints. Finally, their persistence paid off it wasn't until we got into the bathroom and the wall behind the toilet is where we located the Palm prints and fingerprints that were ultimately identified as belonging to Lisa Renee.

So the Palm print itself placing Lisa with them in that same motel room, uh, was very important. It was a very critical piece of, of putting her with them. Investigators now had evidence that Lisa was alive four days earlier, the day Beckley and the others had checked in.

As agents drove the kidnapper 90 miles back to the Eldorado jail. They pressed Beckley for more details. He admitted that after Orlando hauler joined them in Pine Bluff, they decided to move Lisa to another motel nearby in order to avoid a second visit by the security guard.

After a couple of days in that motel, the men grew increasingly concerned about getting caught. They came up with a plan to dispose of the girl. Demetrius hall stayed behind to wipe the room clean while the other three loaded her into Webster's car and headed for a rural area. Beckley told investigators that Bruce Webster and Orlando hall at Dugard greater than a nature preserve near the motel.

They took Lisa there to kill her Mark overgrown park. The three men couldn't find the burial site. After an hour, they took her back to the motel. The next morning they searched for the grave site again.

Well, forensic technician scoured the second motel room for clues investigators, pressured Beckley to tell them what happened next special agent Garrett, Floyd recalls that Beckley refused still afraid that Webster might seek retribution. We were pressed for time because the clock was still ticking. We were hoping against hope that she was still alive.

And so with this in mind, um, agents, as well as police officers who had not slept in two or three days were up searching, looking, hoping that she was still alive.

Then investigators got the call. They'd been hoping for.

The FBI emergency response team working at the second motel had spotted Bruce Webster pull up in his car. This suspected kidnapper had returned to the motel with a young woman, but she was not Lisa Rene.

Brief interview revealed she was not connected to the crime in any way. You're not in any trouble. He had driven up into the parking lot, our officers and the FBI agents confronted him. Um, he identified himself as Bruce Webster gave date of birth information. Uh, he was carrying a small baggie of what appeared to be marijuana in his pocket.

Um, he was asked if we could search his vehicle. He allowed the officers to search his vehicle that he'd driven up in.

Inside the vehicle agents found twine guns.

They charged Webster with possession of the guns in the marijuana and took him to the Garland County jail in hot Springs, Arkansas, the car was processed for other evidence. They found new tricks, the missing girl, and when they read it to us and told us he was in custody. We myself and detective Ford went back and interviewed Bruce Western.

He stated that he didn't know anything. We hadn't done anything wrong. He was simply coming back to his motel room. His agent Floyd continued to pressure Webster for answers. The last of the fugitives Orlando hall turned himself in. Orlando hall had apparently seen the news that these arrests had been made, uh, found out of course, that his brother had been taken into custody.

Uh, he surrendered to the Pine Bluff, uh, police department, all four suspects. Now in custody agents hope that one of them would reveal where investigators could find Lisa Rene. The interview with Bruce Webster, the man who had been hired to do the killing continued into the night, but he said little agent Floyd believed Webster had the answers they were looking for.

Basically the only information Mr. West provided was his name. The fact that he hadn't done anything and the fact that he wanted to go to sleep. So him, it was nothing. She was nothing agent's hope of finding Lisa alive was failing. They needed to get one of the suspects to talk and they needed to do it fast.

Six days after a young woman was abducted from her Arlington, Texas apartment investigators pressed her suspected kidnappers for information, a party until now alleged Hitman.

Bruce Webster had stonewalled investigators, special agent Garrett Floyd's persistence eventually paid off. You can remember nothing else. Webster finally admit it. That Lisa was dead. It felt like a tremendous sledgehammer falling on you. We attract this young lady from Arlington, Texas to Pine Bluff, Arkansas, over 200 miles with the one hope of finding her alive.

Uh, and we did not. Um, it was as if all the wind and all of the energy had gone out of us. Webster picked up the story, whereas accomplished Stephen Beckley left off. When they returned to the park with Lisa, they located the grave. They had dug the day before detective John Stanton's fears had been realized the reality of it set in at that point that we were not going to find her alive.

We were not going to be able to save her. We were going to be too late. Stand by the car. Webster said that only two of his accomplices Orlando hall and Steven Beckley took Lisa back to the park. The fourth kidnapper Demetrius hall had stayed behind it, cleaned the motel, Roman wipe away fingerprints.

This suspected Hitman claimed he wasn't actually with the others when they killed the girl car. Webster said he returned to the car to act as the lookout from the car. The grave was too far away to have seen the murder.

Now that Webster was safely in custody. The agents decided to see if Beckley would corroborate his story. Agent Floyd felt that Beckley knew far more than he had said.

And he looked at me and he said, you know, I didn't tell you everything, you know, I've lied. And I said, yes, I know you did not tell him everything. You didn't lie, but you didn't tell me everything. And he said, you're right. So Dan, Steven Beckley started crying and Steven Beckley told me she was dead, that she was buried in these woods and that we needed to go get her.

And I said, we will go get her. Let's get your story on paper. And we will go and find her. Crazy man. He's a Hitman. Beckley said that despite Bruce Webster's story, the Hitman had indeed been involved in the killing. He told us a story that the grave was six foot deep and that when she went to the grave, when she, um, Bruce Webster, Orlando hall, and he, Steven Beckley arrived at the grave as she saw the grave and that she started to run in the effort to get away.

They struck at her with a shovel and placed a Mark in this tree. That he Beckley became concerned and was afraid and ran back up to discrete to check, to see if the weight was clear as he was instructed to by Bruce

Webster. By the time he came back, they were buried.

Did you ask Beckley told investigators that the men then met Demetrius back at the motel showered and left? They gave their dirty clothes to Webster who burned them in the park. Along with Lisa's bloodstained outfit. Webster stayed in Pine Bluff as Orlando hall while the other two returned to elder rape.

The agent re-interviewed Webster hoping his confession would give him some leverage. The agent told him that Beckley had placed him at the murder scene and named the park where the body was buried.

He stated that he didn't know anything about anything. The last thing that I told him was. Everyone else has told me what it has occurred. Why won't you? And he said, they're family, aren't they? I said, yeah, the family has turned on you. He said, open that book. Let me tell you what happened. The Hitman now confessed that he was in fact at the murder scene.

He admitted that he had dug the grave and he offered to show it to the agent. So when the middle of the night, we drove back to Palm Bluff and told them I need as many flashlights and officers and agents available, that we were going to find her tonight.

To show the investigators, the area of the park, where the body was buried.

They searched for evidence to corroborate the suspect story.

By morning, they found the grave site. They began to process the area and exude the body.

The site was, as the Hitman had described it right down to a damaged tree near the grave.

And we remove a section of that tree. It was evidenced that the shovel that they were hitting her with had actually missed on one of your swings and hit the tree. So we use that tree as a part of the evidence.

Unearthing the body was a time-consuming and heartbreaking process.

Besides digging, investigators sifted through leaves and dirt searching for anything that might help tie the suspect.

Joel Stevenson of the Arlington Texas police recalls the moment when their hard work finally paid off. We made contact with Lisa's body, uh, approximately two feet down from the surface, the outer surface of the, uh, dirt, and then started uncovering her and, and really excavating around the body. From that point on down to the fourth, four feet level.

This lasted for about five and a half hours that it took us to fully extract her from the grave site.

When they reached the dead woman's body. It was an emotional moment for investigators who wanted so desperately to save Lisa Rene.

Doing the time we're exhuming the body. One of the ages on the evidence response team accidentally scrapes her knee. The agent breaks down an operator because we know now that she's dead this week, that we have spent trying to locate her as a result in the recovery of her, but not the recovery of her.

In that she was not alive. The coroner removed Lisa's body to the Arkansas state lab in little rock where an autopsy was performed. She had ligature marks on her arms, defensive wounds on her hands, bruises over much of her body and deep lacerations to the back of her head. But the cause of death was determined to be suffocation coupled with blunt force trauma to the head, the coroner believed Lisa's attackers knocked her unconscious with a shovel and then buried her alive.

When you find out that you were that close to possibly saving, uh, this kidnapped victim from. Her demise as it turned out. Um, it, it, it hurts in that you wish you could kind of go back in time and do something different than you did, but under the conditions that we had and the information we had to work with, we felt like we did as good as we could.

Unfortunately, it wasn't good enough to save Lisa.

The four kidnappers were tried soon after her body was found. Demetrius hall became a witness for the state and accepted a plea bargain of twenty-five years. Steven Beckley did the same and got 30 years Orlando hall received the death penalty for interstate kidnapping resulting in death. A few months later, Bruce Webster received the same sentence, both were sent to death row at the U S penitentiary in Terre Haute, Indiana.

The trials were little constellation to Lisa's sister, Pearl, who could barely absorb the fact that the bright teenager would never realize her dream of becoming a surgeon. I thought that feel better, but I really don't cause it, I mean, it's not going to bring her back then thing. That's going to make it better as Lisa was here today.

And she's, she's not coming back for Arlington police, detective John Stanton. Lisa Rene's murder had disturbing implications. It just solidified the fact that things can happen to people who are completely and totally unrelated to criminal activities. Uh, no one is exempt from the possibility that for no real reason of their own, they get put in a position where their life is in jeopardy.

And Lisa Rene is a prime example of someone that in the years that I've been doing this, she is actually probably the most innocent victim that I've ever worked a case on. And it's, it's something that we all need to remember that even if you're an innocent victim, you can still be a victim for special agent Garrett, Floyd and investigators alike.

The case was personal. I have a daughter. It was approximately the same age as Lisa Renee. And to believe that someone could take a child or a young lady and do the things that they did to her and then kill her without any respectful life takes that father image in me to a different level, because we love our children.

2 UNITED STATES V. JONES

In Minnesota, a gruesome murder left few clues by local drug boss became a suspect, but he was well-insulated against police.

FBI agents and local detectives had to infiltrate a dangerous cartel. Okay, go ahead. And you have to get to a pair of gangsters who killed with no remorse.

Hey burning body in a dark alley shed light on a cold blooded killer. His partners in crime would tell the story. If they live in the underworld of the drug trade, even a childhood friend can quickly become an enemy.

On June 24th, 1990 at about 3:00 AM, the St. Paul Minnesota resident was enjoying the quiet of a summer evening when he noticed a car drive into the alley behind his house.

Moments later, he heard the distinct sound of a fire erupting than the car speeding away.

Checking the alley. He discovered a large object engulfed in flames.

He feared the fire would ignite his property. He called nine one, one

St. Paul emergency units responded when firemen extinguished the flames, they realized it was more than an act of vandalism.

The object was a charred human body wrapped in a melted plastic tarp.

Homicide detectives arrived at the scene.

They questioned the resident, but he hadn't seen the car. Was it

Police found no identification on or near the body?

Investigators hoped an autopsy would provide more information.

If they could identify the victim, it might help lead them to those responsible

The medical examiner determined the victim was a black male in his mid-twenties, and that he was dead before the fire was set

Cause of death, multiple gunshot wounds to the head. The examiner extracted three small caliber slugs, they would be sent to the ballistics lab for examination.

Despite the fire damage, the examiner found powder burns on the victim's head indicating he had been shot at point blank range. If enough of his fingerprints remained, they might help identify him.

The prints were entered into the automatic fingerprint identification system. APHIS is a national database containing the Prince of 23 million persons.

The body had probably been burned to make identification difficult with the APHIS technology. It might be possible. But running the prints would take some time.

Police believed such a gruesome murder was probably drunk related.

Minneapolis St. Paul area had recently become a popular input spot for narcotics

With the drugs, came an increase in violent crime. Special agent John Tyndall of Minnesota Bureau of criminal apprehension, investigated drug running in the area.

The primary way that people moved cocaine into the state at that time would have been through public transportation. That being either by bus or by airplane.

Police created drug and addiction teams assigned to the Minneapolis St. Paul airport to try to stop the influx.

The agents monitored travel to and from cities like Miami and Los Angeles, where the drugs originated.

OnJune 25th, 1990, the day after the body was recovered in the alley, agents were watching the counters where same-day tickets were issued. These two guys approached the ticket agent and stood there for quite some time. Doing what we felt was negotiating the sale of some tickets. They pulled out a wad of cash and they paid cash for the tickets.

They then left the ticket counter.

The agents would check it to counter and learn that the men were flying under the names, Jeffrey, English, and Harry Babs agents caught up with the men at their gate. As they waited to board their flight. They asked if they would answer some questions. We explained to them that they had no obligation to talk to us if they didn't want to, they weren't under arrest.

They were free to leave. Both men consented to be interviewed and said they were just heading back home to LA.

They said, they'd come to St. Paul to visit a friend named Ken Jones by second, or whatever the officers asked for permission to search the bags. They'd checked at the counter.

Both agreed. So a search warrant was unnecessary.

The bags hadn't been loaded onto the aircraft yet inside the one belonging to Jeffrey English was a plastic bag containing rolls of cash totaling $13,000. Alright, got it.

Talk to, into a shoe was a 22 caliber Derringer pistol. It would have been easy to miss. It was a tiny revolver, five round capacity. With a barrel that was only one inch long and the entire gun was approximately four inches long, a gun that could be concealed simply by palming it in your hand.

In the other bag was another handgun. Neither had been declared that violation. Plus the suspicious amount of cash provided enough probable cause for an arrest of was Memorial. The officer radioed his partner, where they could be armed with neighbors. They had to detain Babs in English before they took off

The plane was still at determined.

The agent boarded the plane and found the men already seated. I just need to ask you a couple of questions. In a later interview, English would claim that the money was from selling a car. You said he bought the 22 Derringer on the street in Minneapolis. And he went on to add that he had no idea where the gun had been.

And I thought that was a strange response for a person to back away from the guns history. And that was the first inclination that either of us had that, uh, the gun might've been used in some type of crime. Simply by the way, he framed his response to the question.

Just became more suspicious. When English admitted he was flying under a false name, his real name was Jeffrey barns.

There was no evidence against Barnes or his companion for anything but misdemeanor weapons, violence,

Both men paid fines and were released. Their guns were held until agents could check police records to see if they'd been used in earlier crimes.

Two weeks later, St. Paul police received the fingerprint comparison from the man found burned in the alley.

There was a match from Southern California.

The victim's name was doing on Walker. The 26 year old Los Angeles area resident had a record for intent to sell narcotics.

Walker's desk made the papers in his hometown, his uncle read the article and called the St. Paul authorities

St. Paul police. He told detectives his nephew had gone there to meet a man named Ken Jones. Yes, sir. Thank you very much for your information. We appreciate that. Yes, officer, my name is Lynn Walker. Didn't return from St. Paul. The uncle had contacted Jones, who said Walker had already left. It's going to be a big help.

All right, bye. Bye.

Hold it right here. St. Paul narcotics detectives were familiar with Jones. They had been investigating him for years.

He was reputed to be the largest supplier of cocaine in the region.

Jones was careful with his drug business and well-insulated against investigation. Right? Thanks everyone. On behalf of the public, they donating to urban charities. Ken Jones also portrayed himself as a community. Benefactor police knew it was a cupboard. Like his legitimate businesses, they believe he use to laundry, drug money.

His reputation was different on the street. Yeah. I'm on the dealers and addicts. Jones was known to move his interests with an iron fist. Yeah.

If he didn't get paid, people got hurt.

For years, detectives had been searching for a way to shut the drug boss. Yeah.

It gives you that murder victim do on Walker was with Jones before his death. If they could prove the dealer was involved, they could finally take him off the street, but they needed more evidence.

Investigators went to interview employees of Jones, his business.

They hope someone would know about jones' meeting do on it.

Never seen him before never seen this person at all, but none of the employees were willing to talk drug boss. Ken Jones continued his narcotics trafficking. He seemed to be beyond the reach of the law.

On June 24th, 1990 St. Paul authorities had found the body of 26 year old do on walk burning in and way just before his death. He had met with drug boss, Ken Jones.

Police believe Jones was involved in the murder. But witnesses wouldn't talk and no physical evidence implicated him.

Investigators got an unexpected break. Three months later when St. Paul police stopped a man for a routine traffic violation,

A computer check revealed there was a warrant out for the arrest of Charles shuck.

Yeah, police took him into custody.

They contacted the investigator who had issued the warrant special agent, John Tyndall of the Minnesota Bureau of criminal apprehension.

The arrest warrant was issued for Charles shuck for importing two kilos of cocaine. We, you attempted to find him at the address that he had given and he wasn't there. And we had no way of knowing where he was at that time.

Several months earlier, the drug and addiction team at the Minneapolis St. Paul airport had spotted the courier. Did they watch Chuck pay cash for a full fair, last minute ticket to Los Angeles. That'd be one way. Round trip, round trip route Chuck didn't check a bag and carried only one onto the plane boarding pass here.

The next day agents saw him return now with two bags.

The new couriers often had extra bags when returning from a drug pickup I'm off tomorrow. They told Chuck that they could not arrest him, but they could hold his luggage for inspection.

That's already is, could not open his bags without his consent. And he did not give it

Chuck's response was not that of innocent travelers. If you tell them that you're going to detain their bags, typically if they have nothing to hide, they want to stay with their backs. They don't want to leave those bags behind. Chuck had none of that. He had no questions. He had no concerns. It was his primary concern was getting out of there just as fast as he could.

Shortly after Shaq left a canine unit examined the bags. One was clean.

But in the other, the dog smelled narcotics, can't get a search warrant based strictly on the actions of the dog. The dog was an integral part of it in the request for the search warrant, but it wasn't the only part. We also had to detail the fact that we had seen Chuck the previous night come in by a high dollar. Round trip ticket to Los Angeles with return flight being the following morning.

These things are unusual. The fact that he carried one small bag on the aircraft and carried two off is also unusual. Agents secured a search warrant to open the bags inside. They recovered two kilos of cocaine.

Investigators suspected shuck was carrying the drugs for someone else. At that time, we weren't able to make a connection as to who he might be working with or working for. But my gut feeling was that he was a courier for somebody at a higher level. Now that he had been arrested. Chuck learned of the evidence against him.

He had his attorney proposed exchange for sentencing consideration. He would give up information on the man. He ran drugs.

For importantly, he would also provide details about the unsolved murder of DuJuan Walker.

Chuck said that the man who employed him as a quarrier was the same man who had ordered the murder. The man's name was Ken Jones. For every kilo of cocaine delivered, Ken Jones would pay shuck $1,000. Chuck had worked for the drug Boston's high school. It was precisely because their relationship was so strong.

The Jones did not retaliate for the last cocaine, but Chuck was not the only courier jones' girlfriend also played a major role in the trafficking organization.

Charles shook told me that she was intimately familiar with his drug dealing operation. In fact, she had been a stewardess for an airline for a lot of years and had acted as a courier for him bringing in kilos when she was working as a team stewardess investigators asked Chuck if the girlfriend knew about the murder, basically he said that around the time Walker was killed, she had been very upset.

Irene, are you okay? She told him the Jones had ordered her to clean up the bathroom of his condo was going on. It was a great deal of blood by the bathtub. By the way Chuck had heard Walker had been shot there. He said the killer's name was Jeffrey barns and enforcer for Jones and the same men who suitcase held $13,000 in cash.

And at 22 Derringer pistol that Barnes had shot the victim do on Walker in the head and that left town. The following day after being paid by Ken Jones for that hit shuck alleged that the $13,000 cash that was found in the suitcase was at least part of the hit money that was paid to Barnes by Jones for doing the hit and that the 22 caliber revolver that was found murder weapon.

No, that wasn't my cocaine. I was the shuck knew the caliber of the murder weapon and other details of the crime that hadn't been made public.

So we felt that there was some credibility on Chuck's part that Barnes and Jones could be considered as legitimate suspects in the murder of Walker. Agents realize they might have the murder weapon already in custody. See what we get out of here. Good. Prove it was the gun that killed Walker. They could move forward with a murder case on drug boss, Ken Jones, and his enforcer, Jeffrey barns.

They retrieved the 22 caliber Deringer from the evidence locker.

Investigators sent the Derringer to the St. Paul ballistics lab for testing examiners compared grooved striations inside its barrel to the grooves on the sides, removed from the victim.

But the report is disappointing.

The results were inconclusive in part due to the fact that it only had a one inch barrel and the opportunity to pick up striations from the lands and grooves within this barrel were limited the longer the barrel, the better the opportunity to pick up the striations short barrel. Like this gives you very limited opportunity.

Without a forensic examination matching Barnes, his gun to the bullets that killed Walker. The authorities had only the word of a drug smuggler to bring to trial.

Agents shipped the gun to the alcohol, tobacco and firearms lab in Washington, DC, the feeling was that their laboratory was somewhat more sophisticated. They were accustomed to doing things like that on a routine basis. And with their sophisticated equipment, they might be able to come up with a determination that was more specific after it was examined by ATF.

They came to the conclusion that it was in fact, the weapon that was used to murder do on Walker.

Investigators now knew that enforcer Jeffrey Barnes was in possession of the murder weapon. The day after Walker was killed

But they still had no proof that he had fired the fatal shots or that Ken Jones had ordered the hit.

Get me man agents and detectives sought witnesses who could connect the two men to the homicide. Take a, take a look at the picture. Whether due to loyalty or fear authorities were met with silence.

One after the other, the people we attempted to talk to would not talk to us and they would not give up anything. So we were back to the point of having only the statement given to us by Charles shuck and no palpable way of corroborating into the information that he gave us through other witnesses.

Yeah, come on. Investigators applied for a warrant to search Jones's condominium, but the judge refused to grant one because they couldn't corroborate the story of the blood on the floor and make them the pen registers after almost a year, investigators realized that the case would not be solved without additional resources.

They contacted the St. Paul FBI's drug task force for assistance.

Having worked narcotics for 20 years. Sergeant Tom was well aware of the reputations of Ken Jones and Jeffrey barns. Both of them are very intimidating and opposing individuals. They had a violent background and when we'd go and interview people, everyone would pretty much. Try to avoid either having any contact with us or they wouldn't tell us the straight story.

The task force believed that the only way to get to the drug boss and his enforcement would be through a cooperating witness.

They needed to find someone who could give them firsthand information and perhaps solicit a taped confession. He's a chump. The investigator approached a confidential informant. He had developed on earlier cases.

The informant couldn't place Barnes with the victim, but he did know that the enforcer had a nephew who had recently been released from prison. Okay.

And nephew's name was Russell Barton's known on the street as ice. After leaving prison, he had come to St. Paul to begin dealing cocaine with context provided by his uncle. Jeffrey.

The nephew was anxious to make money, hope to use his eagerness to their advantage.

Investigators developed a new strategy in the fall of 1992.

The enforcers' nephew would become their new target

FBI special agent grant BC. The specialist in wire intercepts was called in as part of the plan. We went after Russell number one, because he was a pretty good sized dope dealer. Uh, number two, he dealt with his uncle Jeffrey and, uh, we felt that if we could, uh, get a case made against Russell that would help us make a case against Jeffrey to get him.

Agents would somehow have to infiltrate the tones of a dangerous drug.

In 1992, investigators believed to St. Paul drug boss and his enforcer had killed on Walker.

They had already recovered the murder weapon,

But Sergeant Tom didn't asking the sign to an FBI drug task force. Needed corroborating evidence in order to arrest drug boss, Ken Jones, and his enforcement Jeffrey barns, just having the weapon alone wasn't enough to get them prosecuted for it. We felt that we're going to have to identify some people or bring some people in to court.

That'll be able to testify at that. Jeff Barnes and Ken Jones were involved in the murder. FBI special agent grant BC believed that if they first arrested the enforces nephew drug dealer, Russell barns, he might provide the information they needed. We had sources of information that, uh, were close to Russell that gave us the indication that he knew, uh, that his uncle had, uh, committed the murder.

We didn't know, to what extent that Russell knew about it,

Right. To build a narcotics case against Russell barns, the FBI enlisted a trusted informant with credibility on the street. And I can hear what I'm saying. Coming back through here, agents wired the informant who would engage in controlled drug buys with the enforcers' nephew.

Task force members would record each by. It was a risky operation. If the informant's wire was discovered, he would likely be killed.

Agents wanted to build trust and avoid any possibility that Russell Barnes might suspect. It was a set-up

Yeah, you won't taste at first, the informant books, and small amounts over time, the transactions increased in size and frequency and each was recorded.

Everything's everything. But Russell Barnes refused to speak about his knowledge of the murder.

Agents were no closer to solving the crime.

The FBI needed to plant someone closer to the enforcer himself.

Dude, in May of 1993, they discovered their way in. And informant working for the St. Paul FBI. On another case, I mentioned that he and Jeffrey Barnes had done time together.

He claimed they were very close and that Barnes trusted him. He said he was sure he could get Barnes to sell him cocaine. And to talk about the Walker, no Barnes really well agents tested the informant's credibility by having him call the enforcer.

Within moments, it became clear. Jeffrey Barnes was comfortable talking to the influence. No, I've been out a couple of months now business. It was the break investigators were looking for now.

They needed to find a place for the drug buys a controlled environment that could be adequately wired. I mean, eating well. Uh, at the time the informant was living with a relative and, uh, couldn't really do things at his home. Uh, we obtained a, uh, a house, uh, from HUD and, uh, moved the informant into the house and the informant agreed to record certain conversations that he might have with Jeffrey barns.

Investigators set the informant up in a government owned house on the West side of St. Paul.

He was to contact the FBI. Anytime the enforcer was planning to visit the house for a drug deal. FBI technicians wired the house with electronic listening devices in three rooms.

Agents new barns like to boast about being a Hitman, referring to himself as murder incorporated.

With that information, we, I tried to encourage the informant to try to bring him to a point where he would talk to him about. You know, acts of violence that he was involved in and things like that. And this is something that Jeff Barnes reputation was all about and something that he liked to brag about agents, coach they're informative on how to draw barns out about the murder of Walker.

He was to lead the enforcer into talking about the hits he performed in the past.

In one tape conversation, the informant pretended he wanted barns to help him Rob a drug dealer.

Jeffrey Barnes suggested that they just kill her. Good. The Hitman alone Barnes told the informant that doing the hit on somebody is not a problem. And he described how he could do it. He would walk up behind the individual, pop them in the head with a handgun, let him fall on the floor. Wrap them in plastic and drag his body outside and put it in an alley.

Um, and this was a, the exact same way that, uh, Walker had been, uh, killed. I won't take up too much of your time. Let's say we get down to business. It was good. Circumstantial evidence that by itself, it wasn't enough.

The buys had been arranged by telephone investigators, secured a warrant to tap the suspect's phone lines.

Oh, the wire intercepts captured no information on the Walker murder. They did produce the tales of the drug operation. In January, 1994, the task force decided it was time to arrest Russell barns and hope he would turn on his uncle.

On January 29th, they set up another controlled drug by, with an informant. It would happen at a downtown St. Paul hotel.

Investigators wired the room for sound. Okay. The reliability, the eavesdropping devices was essential.

Testing one, two, one, two, the recordings would be used in court.

And agents would be monitoring from an adjacent room.

If Russell Barnes discovered the setup, they would be able to protect them. Okay, go ahead and give me a sec. Testing one, two, three. Everyone was ready. They wouldn't have the informant call the enforcers' nephew and order several ounces of cocaine there. He had a little lamb testing. One Mary had a little lamb, Mary investigators in St.

Paul police, special investigations unit. We're conducting the surveillance at Russell Barnes' residence. And after the phone calls were made with very short delay, Russell went to the hotel.

Russell bonds are delivered to the informant. Before I told you one day, we'd be rolling. I see what you mean. He brought cocaine and the equipment he needed for measuring it.

He suspected nothing. To him. It was just another deal.

He set up shop and began the transaction, unaware that every word was being recorded. It was important to get a drug dealer off the streets. But what agents really wanted was for Russell barns to give a statement about drug boss, Ken Jones, and enforcers, Jeffrey barns, committing murder. When details of the drug deal were on tape investigators moved in.

Okay. We're clear. They had indisputable evidence of Russell Barnes selling roughly two ounces of cocaine.

Investigators explained to him that is a three-time narcotics offender. Russell was looking at a minimum of 15 years in prison.

They wanted a statement about his uncle, right? Barnes sat him down and we talked at some length about. Uh, Jeffrey Barnes and his involvement with the Dwan Walker, homicide being somewhat reluctant because this was his uncle. It took some persuasion. And after a while we gained his confidence and he eventually told us his knowledge of about the Dwan Walker home.

Well, Walker, Walden, Jeffrey Barnes had told him, Walker tried to steal cocaine from Ken Jones, took my gun. So they killed him. Huh? The enforcement said they then dumped Walker's body in an alley, doused it with gasoline and lifted a fire.

Nobody messes with me. It was at best a secondhand confession, nobody missing the drug operation. And Russell Barnes was taken into custody. All right, let's go. Agents also arrested their informant. So no one would know he co-opted discovered 22 code. Meanwhile, I'm working on accurate drug boss. Ken Jones was still on the street as was his enforcer Jeffrey barns, but the FBI task force was closing in.

By 1994 while trying to dismantle a Minnesota drug ring and solve a four-year-old murder, the FBI and St. Paul police had arrested dealer Russell Barnes who agreed to cooperate.

He offered details on the crimes, committed by his uncle Jeffrey barns, including nationwide drug trafficking and the 1990 murder of DuJuan

Walker.

According to Sergeant Tom investigators had plenty of evidence against Jeffrey barns, unknown enforcement for drug boss, Ken Jones, the homicide we've got a weapon. That's been recovered at the airport. We've got Jeff Barnes. Making a comment to one of our informants that he, this is how you murder somebody that's adult rip off type of situation, and the actual procedure that he went through when he killed Juan Walker.

And now we have his nephew. Telling us that he's been at his house blood relative that we're going to have testify in court that he actually told him about the murder in August, 1994, investigators staked out the apartment where Jeffrey barns would stay.

They knew the enforcer was offering and willing to kill.

He had no time to react with your hands up on the car. Come on, move. You just did not get charged with murder forward with a drug conspiracy case. Instead, I'm going to be other hand dealing drugs to be XL mate earn Barnes 30 years or a prison.

They would hold the murder case until they had more evidence against him and Ken Jones.

Special agent grant VC believed having Barnes in prison would make witnesses more willing to talk.

Jeff Barnes had the reputation of being an enforcer. He scared people. Uh, we felt that getting him off the street would, uh, take away the intimidation factor, um, against some of these other people. And it would be better, uh, for us to be able to talk to these, these other folks with him being locked up.

The plan worked after Barnes's arrest. Investigators met with an associate of Ken Jones facing a long prison term on drug charges. He offered to be a government witness. He said he had extensive knowledge about Jones's drug cartel and that he had met Dwan Walker just before his murder.

In mid-June, 1990 Jones had ordered the cooperating witness to drive a pickup truck to St. Louis, where he was to meet Walter. The truck had been fitted with a second fuel tank.

Upon arrival in St. Louis do on walkers stuffed several bags of cocaine into the false tank. When full the tank held about 30 kilos of the drug.

That amount of cocaine would have been worth more than a million dollars.

The cooperating witness then drove the truck back to St. Paul, where he turned it over to the drug boss.

Walker had arrived earlier and was staying with Jones at his condominium Jones. Hadn't paid Walker for the drugs yet. In fact, he and his enforcer decided not to. And the two of them can Spire to take the dope and to eliminate the problem and just execute a Dwan Walker. Bo the witnesses testimony would explain the motive for the killing.

He told the agents that several days later he got a call from the drug boss. He was ordered to come over to the condo immediately.

It was Sunday morning, June 24th, 1990. The day following DuJuan Walker's murder. Ken Jones seemed very nervous. He ordered the cooperating witness to get rid of the truck. He had driven up from St. Louis, the one with the false gas tank, the drug Boston man did that. No one be told about the cocaine.

One to two minutes, the witness said Jones, his girlfriend had also told him about cleaning up blood in the bathroom. After the murder, this picture, you recognize this. Do you swear to tell in the summer of 1995, prosecutors convened a grand jury to secure witness testimony under oath?

Jones's girlfriend was subpoenaed to testify, but she denied telling anyone that she cleaned up blood and Jones's basketball never cleaned up any blood. Ken Jones authorities couldn't prove she was lying. They might never be able to indict Ken Jones and Jeffrey barns for murder. No, sir. If you would tell us, please, about in June, 1995 grand jury testimony from odors, prove that one witness perjured herself.

When she denied cleaning up blood in the bathroom of drug boss, Ken Jones, I'm not sure what you're talking about. So on June 21st, the grand jury indicted Jones and his main enforcer Jeffrey barns for the 1990 murder of Duanya Becker.

Barnes the alleged Hitman was already in prison on drug charges.

The day after the indictment, investigators staked out the home of drug boss, Ken Jones,

He had insulated himself well against the investigation. Ken Jones was finally arrested for murder,

FBI drug task force members, Sergeant Tom. He was determined to find physical evidence to back up witness testimony at the trial,

Through the investigation, everything focused on the fact that. Uh, Dwayne Walker was murdered in the bed, in the bathroom, and he was shot in the head there. I was thinking that we may be able to still find a trace of blood in the grounding on the floor, in the bathroom

Euro of criminal apprehension technician's process. The bathroom after Jones was arrested, new tenants had moved into the condo.

They gave their consent for the search.

The technicians tested for the presence of blood using luminol, a relatively new technique at the time, luminol reacts with proteins in blood rendering, my new traces of invisible under ultraviolet light. We were able to determine, and the underlayment. Underneath the tile that there was a significant amount of blood.

They were unable to obtain a DNA off that test, but they were able to obtain a test that showed that it was a significant amount of blood and it was human blood. That was still a traceable back even five years. Mr. Barton and Mr. Joe, it was the evidence investigators needed five. They had on October 31st, 1995, Ken Jones and Jeffrey Barnes went to trial in St.

Paul year, but also for the birder. Okay. Prosecutors outlined what they believed occurred and do on Walker's final hours, but here are responsible for all of this. I delivered roughly 30 kilos of cocaine to Jones.

The drug boss decided he didn't want to pay

At night. He and his main enforcer, Jeffrey barns partied with him Walker, eventually Walker headed into the bathroom.

Jones and Barnes had planned the hit to take place there.

Do one Walker was unarmed.

Barnes fired three shots from his 22 caliber Deringer. As always Jones maintained his distance.

Walker died immediately.

Later that night they wrapped Walker's body in plastic sheets to contain the blood and loaded it into a car.

He drove to dump the body to make identification more difficult. They douse the body with gasoline and set it.

Jones used his girlfriend to cover his tracks after the murder. The bathroom floor was covered with blood, particularly the area around the tub where Walker had fallen.

She was able to clean the surface. The blood had seeped down into the subflooring five years later. Technicians would find it there. You will come away with the inescapable Ken Jones and Jeffrey Barnes with convicted of murder and drug charges for this murder. There has been in March, 1996. They were both sentenced to life in prison without the possibility of parole.

These gentlemen, through the years,

Jeffrey Barnes who had once boasted, he was murder incorporated. Was no longer a threat to those outside the prison system?

Ken Jones had tried to create an image of himself as a community leader. But his greed led to murder and he will never leave prison alive.

3 C-11 SQUAD

In New York in the 1980s, the emergence of crack cocaine brought a new wave of violence, drug abuse, robbed and killed because they scrambled for power. Ordinary citizens were victimized. Isn't children are not immune. The FBI joined forces with the New York City Buicks to take back the streets. Best weapon against deadly drug gangs was the C 11 spot

New York City is no stranger to gang violence, but when a 12 year old child was kidnapped, the gangs had crossed the line Lauren enforcement race to find the missing boy before it was too late. I'm Jim Carlstrom former head of the FBI's New York office agents would have to infiltrate the secret of world of a vicious game to stop the murderous exploits of a drug Lord.

In the 1980s, crack cocaine invaded the Harlem section of New York as it did many urban areas

Over time, cheaper than highly addictive drug crippled communities. Unlike any other drug heads. With the crack came ruthlessly violent gangs that ruled the streets. No one was truly safe

On December 5th, 1989, 12 year old Danelle Porter was walking to elementary school.

He never made it to class the whole day.

When he didn't arrive home after school, his family worried, they hadn't been able to find him in the neighborhood.

At 9:00 PM, then Nell's sister received a phone call, man, on the other end said Darnell had been kidnapped. He wanted $500,000. So the boy would be killed.

The sister said the family didn't have that kind of money. It didn't matter to the color. He warned them not to contact police, then instructed them to go to a restaurant at 120 fifth and Broadway. Behind a trash can in the restaurant. They find something that would prove he was serious. Got it.

A family friend went to the restaurants to the porters, could stay by the phone.

He didn't know if it was a setup.

Following the kidnapper's orders. He checked behind the trash container and found a coffee can.

Inside two rings and audio cassette and a child's severed finger.

Darnell was hurt. It could be bleeding to death. Despite being warned, not to the family called the New York City police. Following you, looking at you, the family told investigators what they knew.

Detectives inspected the evidence.

The sister said that the rings belong to Danelle. They've been given to the boy by his older brother. It's important on the tape recorded plea for help was definitely Danelle's voice. The family told detectives about a second call in which the kidnapper had lowered his ransom to $350,000.

It was still far beyond their means. They said they didn't know why they were targeted for such a high ransom,

But detectives knew what the family wouldn't say came straight back. The victims, older brother, Richard Porter was a major crack cocaine dealer in the area. Police believe the kidnapping was related to his drug empire.

NYP D contacted the New York FBI's reactive squad for assistance.

Special agent David Higgins. Our narcotics expert was asked to provide more intelligence on Richard Porter, Richard Porter. Then about 25 years of age, uh, was a well-known crack dealer. Uh, whose activities took place in central Harlem? Uh, he was one of those individuals who I didn't, I early on the crack trade in New York and he had created a.

A significant drug empire in central Harlem, Richard Porter had made millions of dollars selling crack on New York streets.

Detectives knew where it was turf war going on, man. It didn't take long to find Porter detectives recognize the person he was with because he was drug

This visit wasn't about drugs. It was about finding Danelle

Porter agreed to come to the station for an interview though. He said he didn't know how he could help.

No surprise. I don't know any, maybe at least new portals, very close to that. Now claim to know nothing about who was behind his brother's kidnapping on the streets. These matters are usually solved without the cops.

I don't know. I don't know. No. The Porter most likely held the key finding dunno. He was in no position to talk to authorities, Richard Porter, uh, because of his. Situation as a drug trafficker, uh, found himself in a ticklish situation legally, uh, it would have been difficult for him to cooperate directly with law enforcement.

I believe he attempted to handle this situation on his own. To some extent police had nothing to hold him on.

The authorities needed to find someone else to help them.

They canvas the area, trying to gather information on the kidnapping.

In such a close knit neighborhood, someone had to have heard something about Danelle, but residents were too afraid to talk.

Harlem's violent gangs had a stranglehold on the community.

Detectives were left with nothing with each passing day police in NYP, these 32nd precinct new Danelle's chances of survival decreased. Investigators maintained contact with the boy's family who were desperate. For more words from the kidnapper we need to get to the bottom of the week. After the abduction, the family received a note, the kidnappers hinted Danelle was still alive.

They demanded their money. But no more ransom calls came with no clues to the boy's whereabouts and no one talking police had reached a dead end. They somehow needed to pressure Richard Porter, Andrew co-op. You got to give him back or hope he would pay the ransom to get Danelle back.

Then on January 4th, 1990 a month after Danelle's abduction the body of his brother. Drug kingpin. Richard Porter was found in a Bronx park. He had been shot twice in the head and chest. There would be no one to pay the ransom. Now it was widely assumed that Richard's death was connected to, uh, the kidnapping and probably the result of it.

Ransom payment combat. However, it was noted early on that, uh, when his body was discovered, uh, his wallet contained over $2,000 in us currency. Uh, his jewelry was there. Uh, apparently his automobile was nearby. Uh, so there was some question about what the actual motivations were behind his murder with Richard Porter's death investigators lost their closest connection to the abducted 12 year olds.

To find another source. They increased pressure on lower-level dealers in Porter's organization, facing drug charges.

They were offered leniency in exchange for information, some said Porter's partner, Albo Martinez could be involved.

Others claimed an intimacy column gang called the preacher crew might be offered direct leads to the crime.

Three weeks later, a boy's body was recovered in the same Bronx Park where Richard Porter was found to dynamic his family identified the body of Danelle Porter.

Cause of death was blunt force trauma to the head.

A death of a child is always a disturbing event. Um, there was a 12 year old boy he's on the way to public school. He's kidnapped, uh, tortured. Uh, he's heard, uh, on the tape cassette, uh, crying for help from his family, the Nell's murders, stunned the entire Harlem community, even though violence was a daily occurrence.

At the time Sergeant James Marr worked in YPD is notorious 32nd precinct where Danelle lived the eighties and the early nineties, 32nd precinct, which is actually geographically, only one square mile was one of the most violent precincts in New York City. Um, they averaged in the area of the upper sixties to low seventies of, uh, homicides a year and added on to that were shootings several hundred shootings that the people didn't die in response to the increased violence in the city.

A taskforce called the C 11 squad had been formed at the FBI's New York field office.

Detectives from the 32nd precinct and FBI agents were assigned to the squad was created to address these entrenched criminal conspiracy groups in the city of New York. The locals brought their knowledge of the streets. Uh, the knowledge of the subjects involved to the table. Uh, the federal agents brought along with them, the access to the federal courts, um, which included the access to the federal sentencing guidelines in the United States attorney's office.

After the murder of Danelle Porter, they knew they had to take back the streets C 11 would first go after Albo. Martin is Richard Porter's partner. The problem is here. Their partnership had unraveled. He would have had the most to gain from extorting rigid pork and killing him, still working on some surveillance a year earlier, a warrant had been sworn out for his arrest on drug charges, but when Martin has couldn't be found, federal prosecutors had to drop the warrant in police computers, the C 11 squad flag.

The names of known associates of Albo Martin is if any were arrested, they would be notified.

Police in Washington, DC pulled over a car after observing its driver engage in a drug.

The driver was a known courier for ALPA Martin.

Police found a large amount of crack and thousands of dollars in his car. Noting the flag on his record from New York, DC authorities would contact the C 11 squad.

After the courier was sentenced to 20 years to life on drug charges, C 11 agents had him transported to New York for an interview. I want some internet, an agent explained that under federal law, his sentence could be reviewed if he cooperated with authority.

Drugs would be distributed both in New York city by Richard Porter and in Washington, DC by ALPA Martinez while in Washington, DC Martinez allied himself with individuals that he. Uh, found to be strong on the street, if you will, in order to protect his drug operation in Washington, DC. And it was not unusual for literally sea bags worth of us currency to be shipped out of Northern Virginia and Washington DC up into, uh, the

Porter neighborhood at 130 second and seventh Avenue in New York city.

It was enough for a renewed arrest warrant on APOE Martin.

Agents canvas the neighborhood, talking to people who knew Mark.

Most were afraid to talk. Eventually agents learned the fugitive. Who's going to pick up his wife's car at a dealership in Northern New Jersey.

Undercover agent staked out the dealership.

They didn't know if Martinez would show up, but they knew he liked fast cars.

That afternoon, a sports car.

They watched a passenger get out, but it wasn't Martinez.

Agents couldn't tell if the fugitive was driving,

They had to risk a closer look. If they could arrest Martinez, it might help solve the murders of Richard Porter and his 12 year old brother L an agent visually identified Martinez as the driver. He radio to go ahead signal before the arrest team could respond. Martin spun away.

Agents gave chase, but the fugitive disappeared into heavy traffic.

With Albo, Martin is still a fugitive, the abduction and murder of 12 year old Darnell Porter remained unsolved

The abduction and murder of 12 year old Darnell port showed that Harlem's drug violence was out of control. The FBI C 11 squad knew the murder was connected to the boy's brother crack dealer, Richard Porter, but Porter himself had been killed C 11, believed finding Porter's partner Alfa Martinez would provide answers, but in 1991, Martin has had alluded an FBI undercover operation.

From the incident, the FBI got his license plate number and alerted New York police to be on the lookout for the vehicle. The next day, police spotted it parked on a Harlem street. They impounded it, hoping it might lead to Martin means they believe the fugitive wouldn't retrieve the vehicle himself, but FBI special agent David Higgins waited to see if he'd send someone or young ladies showed up, who claim to be the true owner.

She was the registered owner. Um, ultimately a quick investigation established that, uh, she was a, what we call a straw man or somebody who had stepped forward in order to buy and register the car. On behalf of, uh, Mr. Martin Martinez was nowhere to be found in New York, acting on a tip that he had traveled to Washington DC.

Agents set up surveillance at the DC home of the fugitives. Ex-wife in the early hours of November 7th, 1991. They spotted Martin as getting into his ex-wife's vehicle. This time he wasn't driving. As they pulled out, the FBI made them

The fugitive's ex-wife pulled over.

The cocaine in his possession helped cement the case against one of the biggest drug traffickers on the East coast.

Ultimately, uh, Mr. Martin has pled guilty to an indictment in the Eastern district of Virginia, which accused him of trafficking and over a thousand kilograms of cocaine. Uh, the wholesale value of that. Would be a $20 million.

Investigators also had evidence against modernism on several gang land murder. I don't know nothing about, they told him they knew he was Richard Porter's partner. So he stood to gain from Denelle's and Richard's death. Okay. Hoping to avoid the death penalty. Albo Martin has agreed to cooperate.

He admitted killing his partner, Richard Porter, just like we always do on the weekend. Martinez had begun to suspect his partner had been cheating him out of hundreds of thousands of dollars. From there. He said that more than a year earlier on January 4th, 1990, he and an associate had taken Richard Gordon for a ride almost immediately. Martin is, and the associate each shot.

They dumped his body in the Bronx Park where it was found the next day.

Martin has sworn it was just about missing drug money.

It had nothing to do with Darnell Porter's kidnapping and murder, no evidence or testimony linked Martin to that crime.

He went to prison for life.

Although they had put away a major drug dealer, the local and federal investigators of the C 11 squad were no closer to solving the murder of Darnell

They reviewed FBI intelligence already gathered on other Harlem gangsters who might've profited from extorting and killing Richard Porter.

One gang stood out is likely suspect

They were known as the preacher crew, the gang's leader was Clarence pincher.

Heatley FBI special agent Joe Walsh, formerly of the C 11 squad knew the preacher and his crew were well entrenched and very dangerous. Preacher crew was the established cruel neighborhood, uh, you know, for a long time, uh, preacher bank kicking around the streets of home since the early seventies. And, uh, everybody knew him by his nickname, the black hand of death, and everybody was definitely afraid of him.

N Y P D Sergeant James Mar of the C 11 squad learned the preacher had a reputation for violence, but the gangster was an elusive figure in Harlem. You could walk up to anybody in a 32nd precinct, no matter how church-going they are. No matter whether they're businessmen or local drug dealers, they all have a preacher story.

They all know who preacher is. Ask any of them to describe, preach it to you. Or majority of them, they're not going to be able to, because this guy was an infamous legend in all the players in Harlem's drug underworld had carved up the area into zone. Each block. Each alley was the established turf of a single dealer.

Most dealers respected the boundaries, but the preacher did not. He considered all of how his turf, he made his money, not by dealing drugs. But by texting other dealers, it was mostly into extortion, extorting drug deals. These are guys that were violent in their own, in their own. Right. He would go up and claim their car. If a drug dealer looked like he was getting paid. So to say he was driving a brand new full-size Mercedes-Benz and preach it like that car. That was preachers.

Those who argued with preacher paid a heavy price. It was a system that made him a rich man. You're hitting every other drug dealer on the streets, you know, 2000 hair, 3000 half, 5,000. And that's a lot of money in ads up and believe me, they all paid because if they didn't pay, Peter would pay him a visit or he would order his people to pay him a visit and they'd wind up dead.

The preacher's history of extortion and violence made him a likely suspect in the abduction and murder of Danelle poet. John C 11 had outlined the basic structure of a preacher crew, including, uh, some of those other main guys. The preacher's main Lieutenant was a man named John cuff.

He was a particularly dangerous criminal according to see Eleven's detective Vinny Flint. John cuff was an ex New York City housing cop as a cop. Uh, he provided, uh, protection and bodyguard work for a preacher. Um, so if they were driving through the neighborhood and was stopped, uh, John cuff had a shield where he would probably be, uh, let go and not given a summons or anything further, what happened?

Um, John cuff had a reputation of wanting to be feared a very violent person. Hey Don, for a change, we've got no evidence linked either man to Donald Porter. Those C 11 suspected preacher was involved in the deadly kidnapping, right? He probably didn't commit it himself.

Brad's payday. He distanced himself from most of the crimes having his main Lieutenant and other henchmen carry out his orders.

Features command they're brutal extortion tactics and the money and kept witnesses too intimidated to talk effectively, insulating the crew against investigation.

We went to a, you know, a bodega, you know, someplace up in Holland and we'd say, we know he came in here and. Well, the guy would have a cast on his hand. We know he broke your hand and, and the shop owner was saying, I don't know what you talking about, you know? And that, that shop owner would be paying rent, you know, or taxed and the preacher, but nobody would tell us anything with people too afraid to talk crimes, continue to pile up on new year's Eve, 1992 emergency units responded to a call in the preacher's territory.

A man lay dead in his car, the victim of a drive by shooting his family survived the howling ordeal. They described how the killers pulled up next to them on the street and opened fire.

They claimed they didn't know who did it or why. And like the Nell's kidnapping, no one in the neighborhood admitted, seen anything. It was another tragic killing in Harlem that might go unsolved.

The C 11 squad had to breach the area's violently enforced code of silence. And finally get insiders to talk. A shocking drive by shooting was added to the list of unsolved murders in Harlem.

With witnesses too afraid to cooperate with the police. The case was open for two years. Then in 1994, the C 11 squad found a witness who told them the shooter was a preacher crew member named Malique.

Detective Vinny Flynn learned that Malik had a violent reputation. He became a so-called director of security for the preacher organization. Uh, he was in charge of the group of members who were known as the janitors. The janitors were the people that had to clean up. The problems with the mess of the family and you couldn't be a janitor unless you killed somebody to get more on the leak.

And the preacher group C 11, tried to send in undercover officers.

It was yet another dead end, according to FBI special agent Joe Walsh. We weren't able to, uh, really get in, so to speak and get an undercover in there to buy, uh, narcotics from preacher because preacher was very, very careful. He was a, you know, he's a very smart man and we couldn't get the, uh, the undercover, you know, close to him.

The preacher had closed ranks, ordering the people. They extorted not to sell to new buyers and to keep a low profile on the street.

Investigators needed a witness with close ties to the car.

They distributed business cards, hoping one would find its way to an insider, willing to talk.

Their persistence paid off

April, 1994, a crew member contacted the C 11 squad because he realized his life was okay in danger.

You said the preacher had started going after his own crew members, probably preacher had killed two of the informant's partners. Could I take a look at some pictures? Fairing? He was next. He asked Sergeant James Marr for protection. It was a stone cold killer himself who became an informant. That was so fearful of preacher and of being killed, like as part in his head that he came to me, that he came to us, that he gave us information on specific crimes that he talked about crimes that had been unsolved for years.

Investigators were frustrated that the informant knew nothing of 12 year old Danelle Porter's kidnapping and murder, but he did give investigators their first specific insider information about Peacher Hedley's organization.

He mentioned, uh, killing basements that the crew used as a meeting place and execution chain.

Talk to me at some meetings, Pete, you would call for a vote on the fate of gang members who had fallen out of favor killer. If the majority voted thumbs down, preacher ordered an. In March, 1994, preaching called for a vote on the leak. The janitor who had done the drive by shooting, he believed Malik could no longer be trusted.

The vote was thumbs down.

Reaches summon Malique to head forms.

Malique thought he was there to take part in the beating of a crew member that he had had problems with in the past. All right. Not realizing that he was the real target. Malique was excited and others invited him to the basement.

If you went down there and you were followed in there, you know, somebody who's behind you, you want coming out alive.

He had to die. Was gaining too much influence within the organization, preacher pleaded for his life, but the order had been given.

Clean him up preacher's command. Other janitors used a circular salt to dismemberment.

The informant said that preacher ordered him and another crew member to dispose of the body parts.

They poured acid on Maleek's arms to remove gang tattoos that could link him to the crew. Then they left the body parts and several crumbling abandoned buildings. So you, I kept my head, you know, um, and a refrigerator for a couple of weeks, uh, and they kind of parade it around on a stick. You know, that's how preacher would, you know, uh, keep the fear of, uh, fear of God, so to speak in the, uh, in the younger, younger Turks in his organization.

The fear was too much for the informant though. We knew leaving the crew was equivalent to a death sentence. I hope to see 11 squad could protect now.

It didn't take long for word to get back to the preacher that the informant had cooperated.

One day the informant was leaving a New York courthouse when he spotted preacher in cuffs

He was sure they were there to abduct and kill him.

He went to his car and called his C 11 handlers.

The informant advised me that his fear that he was going to be killed by the organization. He was going to be abducted. Right in the middle of the afternoon, as far as the courthouse,

The agents of CLF rushed to stone, another murder in the preachers,

A former member of the preacher group. Feared the gang was out to kill him for cooperating assault.

Jensen detectives from the FBI C-level squad came to his aid just in time.

They arrested main Lieutenant John cuff and the crew leader himself. Clarence preacher Heatley.

Sergeant James Mark, and the other arresting agents searched the vehicle.

There was evidence inside, including information about my informant masks tape. There was a parent at the time that my informants, um, feelings were right. He was going to be abducted that day. Come on, man, hurt my butt. No one could prove that the men were coming to kill the informant 20 minutes and all that stuff.

The preacher and cuff were released. Incident brought the, see 11 squads investigation of the crew into the Oakland.

That's what it became apparent that they were being investigated by the FBI. I mean, here's this detective that they know from the three to then when he does make an arrest makes arrest with FBI agents, it became apparent to coffin preacher that the FBI was breathing down their neck.

You're further insulated himself. The FBI would have to get him by going after his organization to prosecute. They would use federal racketeering statutes known as Rico. Originally designed to bring down organized crime families, Rico requires that strict criteria are met according to FBI special agent Joe Walls.

You have to have your organization. You have to have your leader, which in this case was preacher. And he has to have five or more people working underneath him, you know, facilitate, uh, the conspiracy of the organization. But you also need three predator, defenses, three federal offenses. See 11 investigators surveilled the preacher crew gathering evidence on offenses to support the Rico case.

They noticed unrest within the gang.

It seemed the pressure of investigation was getting to the preacher. From an informant agents learned, he even ordered the murder of his main Lieutenant, John Cuff.

Agents were obligated to warn cuff of the hit.

I reach my shield. He goes, I know who you are and you don't have to show me your shirt. I said, no. John is wanting to let you know that, uh, there's a contract out of your life. And I swear there's nothing but space. When you look in his eyes and he goes, everybody wants me dead.

Cuff was undaunted by the threat.

Though the preacher was tightening his grip on his men, investigators still needed to get evidence of the crimes, the crew committed to support the racketeering organization.

As more buyers and sellers were arrested, some of helping to outline the group in detail, according to detective. Yeah. We obtained the informants through, uh, narcotics investigations arrests made by, uh, the three, two precinct and the three, two detective squad, uh, through information they developed and informants, they developed.

Um, because of arrest, uh, information was compiled, which built a case against, uh, the preacher. What murders do you know about? Unfortunately, no one had information on the Danelle Porter murder.

One arrested crew member offered details of another murder, committed by the crews, hoping for leniency. He said they decided they didn't want to pay for a shipment of drugs. They told the supplier that a young woman had stolen them and that they would take care.

She was a single mother who sometimes worked as a courier for the crew.

They brought her to a Harlem apartment telling her they wanted her to hear a record. They had produced it up.

She hadn't stolen any drugs

That didn't matter to the crew.

The informant explained how they cleaned up the crime scene, the body in an abandoned building. He couldn't remember exactly which building it was.

In August, 1996, after more than five years of meticulous investigation, us attorney's office of the Southern district. Decided they had enough for indictments and arrests on federal weaker. All right. The first indictment was against Clarence preacher Hateley and John cuff indictment was kept seeing if word got out to the preacher, he might disappear forever. Investigators staked out preacher's Harlem headquarters.

They hope news of the indictments hadn't been leaked and that if they found him, they could arrest him without a fight. They knew preacher was surrounded by men, willing to kill his command.

In late 1996, the C 11 squad was ready to arrest Clarence preacher. Heatley no one had seen him in days.

On August 12th, he emerged from his headquarters building. Detectives made sure he was alone. Then moved in.

As he was arrested, the elusive gang leader remained relaxed and calm. Yeah.

As soon as he was in custody, other teams arrested his main Lieutenant John cuff,

Two months later, 15 more pre-approved members were indicted.

The simultaneous tape.

I had to strike fast, full force to arrest gang members safely. Detective Vinny Flynn and other C 11 investigators developed more cooperating witnesses among the arrested crew members. Once people well were arrested and being prosecuted, they agreed to cooperate and they, uh, felt that they were used by the preacher crew and felt that if in some cases, if they didn't.

Uh, participate, they would have been killed too. So this was, um, they are way out, uh, of the preacher crew and from under, uh, Clarence Wheatley's control investigators learned in which Harlem buildings, the crew dumped some of their victims, finding physical evidence was crucial in order to prosecute the Rico case.

One building was a shell partially collapsed on the inside for the complicating things. After days of excavating, tons of rubber of body was discovered. Lab examiners determined. It was the body of the young mother who had been killed as a cover for stolen.

She had been shot in an apartment in an adjacent building.

Evidence response teams check the apartment.

That's the apartment where they kept the money shed. And in the refrigerator, there was a lot of blood still left in the apartment. And inside the refrigerator, there was malicious blood from when he, when he kept his head, they were able to, uh, trace out at the land Malique and several others had been killed in the basement of the preachers headquarters.

Crime scene technicians processed. The basement arrested crew members said preacher had them scrubbed the place with boric acid. After each killing, most of the basement was clean, but technicians were able to recover traces of blood on the windows and on the saw blade that had been used to dismember Malique.

But the investigation was not over the abduction and murder of young Darnell Porter was still unsolved. Good morning, gentlemen, have a seat answers about his death.

Finally came from an unlikely source, an assistant district attorney convinced the boys preach a crew member, John . Come in to talk for driving. Right. Well, let me through, he was one of the crew's main players left on the street and had been labeled a snitch. Two attempts have been made on his life because you want to take business by DL suggested that Porter cooperate to earn protection in prison.

He confessed to several murders and revealed what happened to his nephew. Danelle. According to Sergeant James Marr, the kidnapping was prompted by jealousy and greed. The underlying factor with Johnny Porter, Johnny apples with the kidnapping was when he came home from prison, Richie Porter, his nephew was this big Harlem drug dealer.

He was getting paid. Richard Porter used to wear a lot of gold used to really like flashy cars. He was making a lot of money and he wasn't giving any to Johnny Porter and Johnny Porter felt he was owed this and he decided to take it. And the way he was, he took it as he snatched the kid. Porter said the preacher agreed to the kidnapping.

He sent one of his janitors Malique to help. They believed Richard Porter would pay anything to get his brother back.

No, they kept the boy in a basement where no one would hear it.

They cut off his finger and recorded the boys, please, for help to prove to his family, they were serious.

Pull in preacher hope for $500,000 enough to set Apple up in his own drug trade and enough to cripple Richard Porter. What time was it when Richard couldn't come up with that amount of cash, they lowered it to $350,000.

Then the unexpected happened, preacher, in Apple learned that Richard Porter was murdered.

There'd be no ransom show about that. Make the creature Heatley later told special agent Joe Walsh about his decision shot right down on the room. And, uh, and told me exactly what happened. Um, you know, uh, he looked me right in the eye and said, you know, I couldn't let that boy live after, uh, after what had happened.

John Porter insisted that it was Malique who actually did the killer. Malique was later killed and dismembered at the preacher's command.

John Porter was sentenced to natural life.

Because of the evidence collected by the C 11 squad, each member of the preacher crew went to their leader, Clarence preacher, Heatley pled guilty to federal racketeering charges that included drug, trafficking, assault, and murder. He was sentenced to life with no chance of parole. He and his crew will never, again. Terrorize the streets of Harlem. It's estimated that they're responsible for approximately 45 murders that we're aware of numerous robberies. If you add the extortion in these people were, were a decade long or better crime wave in themselves, they were, they were just amazing. The devastation that they caused in these communities. That changed when the C 11 squad dismantled the preacher crew for, since the case was closed, Harland has seen a rebirth call them today.

4 THE COFFEE SHOP MURDERS

In July, 1997, triple murder terrified capital. Investigators could find no immediate suspects and no clear motive for the attack. Metro DC police turned to the FBI. They hope the Bureau's technical expertise could bring justice to the victims of the triple homicide.

They Georgetown coffee shop in Washington, DC. Three employees was shot to death. Evidence at the crime scene pointed in many different directions. Was this a hate crime, a robbery gone wrong, or an active cold blooded vengeance against one of the victims?

What seemed at first to be a senseless act of violence soon grew into a crime of federal proportions.

In 1997, Washington DC and its monuments played host to thousands over the three day 4th of July weekend. Visitors attended Independence Day celebrations throughout the Capitol.

By Monday morning, July 17th, the holiday was officially over habit. And so the Georgetown section of DC, we're just waking up to face the workweek five 15, the day shift supervisor at a popular coffee shop arrived to prepare for the onslaught of rush hour. She was surprised to see the night manager's car in the party.

The shop should have been closed at 8:00 PM. The previous night she found the light still on the music playing and fresh pastries behind the counter yet. No one seemed to be there in the shop. Hadn't been thoroughly cleaned.

You check the shift schedule to see who was working the night before

Katie, Katie, she headed toward the back room, searching for her colleagues and some sort of explanation there. She found the slaughtered bodies of the night crew. Oh, my God, the first beautiful city bus driver called the police.

Yeah.

Bye Dawn, the DC metropolitan police had sealed the shop and began to process the scene.

A shoe print found by the front door did not match the souls of any of the victims nor the day manager, employees were killed by multiple gunshots.

Night manager, Katie Mahoney, age 24, 18 year old, Aaron David Goodrich and Emory Alan Evans, age 25.

The victims had apparently been caught in the middle of their cleanup routine sometime after closing at 8:00 PM. Katie Mahoney, who sustained most of the gunfire. Was apparently still holding her keys when she fell to metropolitan police, detective James, train them, the ones in violence seemed like an act of personal vengeance.

When I first learned. Of how the bodies were positioned in the number of shots that had been inflicted on Katie. Uh, one of the, one of the initial theories was, was it was a domestic that she had had a fight with a boyfriend and ex-boyfriend the other two were in the back room, giving them some privacy.

She had gone to the back. Followed by the boyfriend and there, and he exploded, shot her multiple times and then shot them as they tried to come to her assistance. Six spent casings and four slugs from a three 80 semiautomatic were collected from the floor in the ceiling, over the safe. They discovered one of three slugs from a 38 revolver.

Multiple shots from two different guns suggested at least two gunman, detective train him now theorized that it might've been a robbery bottle horribly. When we found out that there were two guns and that there was a shot to the ceiling above the safe, which is typically a warning type shot, then that's when we started looking at commercial robbery.

Now, was it totally conclusive that that made it a robbery? No, absolutely not. If it was a robbery attempt, the gunmen had likely panicked since they left empty handed, the cash drawers were untouched and there were no signs. The safe had been tampered with the receipt, showed that one of the employees purchased a pound of coffee at eight 40.

Which meant they were likely still alive. 40 minutes after the shop had closed.

Detective spoke to one witness who stopped by the shop at about nine 15 previously. I saw the two male employees inside cleaning. The door was locked. So he left assuming it was closed. Several other would be customers told detectives that they had visited the store moments later at around nine 30, nine 30.

We had actually two groups of people independently walk up to the front door. The door was unlocked. They walked right on in. They looked around, they could see that the store was in the process of being cleaned up, but there was nobody there. So they figured that people were in the back and they left at that time.

So we figured based on that sort of information that the murders occurred between nine to 10 and nine 30, the day shift manager told the detective that when she arrived in the morning, the front door was locked. The back door had been locked as well. There was no way to lock them without a key. If it was an inside job, she had a good idea of who it might be. One of the first things she told us about was an ex-employee who had been fired just a few weeks before that he, uh, had a drug habit.

He had, and he was a shift manager. So he had access to the safe to the alarms. The night after the theft, Katie noticed a discrepancy in the cash drawers on her shift.

She tracked the loss to a single employee and fired him.

The company did not press charges against Amanda and he agreed to pay back what he took over time.

Police interviewed the ex-employee. It is Georgetown home. He explained that he and Katie had worked out a payback agreement for the money he owed.

He claimed to Harbor no bad feelings towards her. Investigate his photograph, the soles of his shoes to compare against the print, recovered at the crime scene.

They provided no match. You said he was out of town at the time of the murders. His alibi checked out. Thank you. The viciousness of the slayings became clearer at the autopsy. Katie Mahoney had been shot five times.

Emory Allen Evans had been shot three times. Aaron David Goodrich had been shot once the bullet piercing, both lungs and his heart slugs removed from the victims confirmed that two weapons had been used. The unsolved murders, riveted the public's attention. We are deeply saddened by the loss of three partners. Married. These are the coffee shop chain offered a $50,000 reward for information leading to them. Marie Evans, also a barista,

Some believed it was a hate crime against the minority victims. Others claimed it may have something to do with Katie's former internship at the white house. What seemed more likely was that one of the victims may have been an accomplice who was double-crossed after giving access to the killers. The fact that no money was taken did, uh, increase the number of possible theories as to why.

And actually what happened inside the store, uh, but I think that once we did look into the background of the employees, once he found out what type of people they were that began to eliminate a lot of the theories, maybe Katie was supposed to, to help focus the investigation. The detective called on his friend from the FBI Washington field office, special agent, Brad Garrett.

Over the years, detective training had come to rely on agent Garrett's expertise. I've had a lot of experience in analyzing crime scenes, doing victimology, studying offender characteristics. And so it's, it's sort of like another set of eyes looking at, uh, at a scene. You know, there's nothing magical about it, but, um, I think Jim respects my opinion and asked me initially to come take a look.

The next day, investigators returned to the coffee shop to search for more clues. They noted the store had no security cameras and its alarm had not been breached the night of the crime, the front lock functioned properly and showed no signs of temporary. Perhaps the killers attended with a key, since the door was locked.

After the murders, the investigators tried to piece together events with what little they knew. They figured that the crew was still cleaning the store just after nine 15. That's when the killers must have burst in immediately. The gunmen probably hustled the crew into the back room, closer to the safe.

This is where they had apparently lost control of the situation. The bullet hole in the ceiling, looked like a warning shot designed to get attention.

Shout out to the ceiling. Definitely closed space. Probably only increased everyone's panic. Resulting in this triple tragedy, couple of rounds, investigators concluded that robbery not murder was likely the gunman's initial intention. They also believed that perpetrators had robbed before and would do so. Again, it's fairly rare in robbery situations where they kill the patrons or the employees of the store. So I wasn't really looking at groups that had killed other people.

I was looking at groups that came in guns drawn, were ready to commit violence if they needed to commit violence. So, and again, that's not uncommon for people in, uh, in robberies obviously to pull guns out, but typically people that will Rob a commercial facility like this coffee store. Um, well, typically the target similar type situation, but the scenario presented few clues to the killers, identities, investigators hoped and overlooked answer remained in the shop behind the counter.

The detective found Katie Mahoney's to do list. She had almost completed it. The night she was killed. One item she hadn't checked off yet was to apologize to an employee.

Detectives learned that Katie had reprimanded the employee for his less than professional appearance. A few days before she was killed, the man said that he bore no grudge gets kicked. I was just shooting. So we were doing, you explained that she was sensitive and might've felt concerned that she'd been too harsh with him, but he didn't feel that way. Don't drive. Okay. All right. Investigators confirmed. He was with friends when the murders took place, it was another dead end check out.

Detective training poured over store procedures and policies, and discovered that someone else had been to the store at 2:00 AM. We found out that the pastry guy comes with his, you know, delivery. When he arrived there that morning, he just assumed that the door was locked, used his key, push the carts and closed and locked it behind.

And that's how come when the shift manager got there all the time doors were locked. The pastry delivery explained why the front door had been locked, but it did not reveal how the killers gained entry. Three days after the triple homicide investigators still had no leaves to the killer's identities, the murderers were still on the loose.

On July 7th, 1997, three employees had been shot to death in a Georgetown coffee shop. A reward offered by corporate headquarters and local businesses. For information grew to $100,000. The largest for a crime in DC history, heavy publicized reward, induced dozens of false claims. Special agent Brad guarantee, chasing rumors as part of the job.

One thing you have to do in any of these cases is you have to keep a lot of balls in the air at the same time. You can't just do one thing. So while we're looking at the backgrounds of the victim, disgruntled employees, employees that have been fired, we're also looking at robbery groups. We're also talking to robbery, homicide detectives in the metropolitan area about what cases they've had.

Is there anybody that sort of fits this John era of? Of what happened despite their efforts. They found no leads after two and a half months. Then on September 27th, 1997, metropolitan homicide detectives received an anonymous call call it claim that two people involved in the shooting. One was named Carl didn't know Carl's last name, but described him as thin mid-twenties with Brown skin.

According to detective James, train him. He said, Carl lived on Gallatin Street, describe the location where he lived. And he said he lived there with his mother, his wife and his child, and that they drove a car that was a different color blue. They said, if anybody is telling you anything else, they're wrong.

Your name, sir, the man promised to call back trainee. Just got some good information. Investigators check DMV records and assembled a list of all the cars on Gallatin Street in Washington, DC on the 1200 block, one registered to a man named Carl Cooper. The car was listed as blue criminal background check revealed a 28 year old. Carl Cooper had a record of commercial armed robbery and suspected murder. Carl Cooper and an associate Rob two convenience stores at gunpoint in Prince George's County, Maryland in January, 1989.

When Cooper's associate was later found shelter desk Hooper was the prime suspect. The police never found enough evidence to prove he killed his partner.

His criminal record coupled with the anonymous caller statement made Carl Cooper, the prime suspect in the coffee shop. Triple homicide investigators needed to find out more about Cooper, special agent Brad Garrett, secured a warrant to establish a trap and trace on Cooper's home phone. A pin register and track and trace would give you incoming and outgoing telephone numbers.

Only. You cannot hear what goes on the line, but it records every time you dial a number out, we get, it shows up on a screen and every time someone calls into you, it shows up and it shows up, it shows the duration of the call. So what that did, obviously it gave us who Mr. Cooper was talking to what individuals out there in the community.

Is he interacting with agents discovered that one man worked as a local barber called Cooper's home frequently informants claim. The barber was likely Cooper's accomplice in the coffee shop killings.

Gather more information on Cooper and those who visited undercover agents dressed as telephone, repairmen, and set up surveillance on Carl Cooper's house.

We'd put up a very discreet whole camera outside his house where it would shoot 24 hours a day on his front door. To see, obviously who's coming and going. What hours does he keep? What is his routine? What cars does he get into? Who comes to visit him? Agents didn't need a court order since it was public surveillance.

They monitored Cooper around the clock and created a videotape record of everyone entering and leaving the house.

Anyway, they identified his child. And his wife, the surveillance was not limited to his home. Teams were also assigned to tail Cooper throughout the city. Carl Cooper visited the barbershop, whereas alleged accomplice worked.

Investigators needed to somehow confirm if the Barbara had been involved in a coffee shop killings, they hoped to trap and trace on his phone would tell them more at this point, we're just trying to figure out that this guy is in the barbershop. And what is his relationship with Carl and had he committed robberies with Carl?

So we did a background on him. He had served time for armed property. And based on what sources were telling us that the two of them. Along with other individuals. Hey, committed, armed properties. Agents discovered a stronger connection through the trap and trace on the barber's form. Recognize the name of a woman who called the Barbara frequently.

She was the former girlfriend at the robbery partner, allegedly killed by Cooper several years earlier.

She said that Cooper and the barber and her boyfriend at the time were all friends before her boyfriend was killed. Now, she only kept in touch with the bomb since she believed Cooper was responsible for her boyfriend's death. She also knew Cooper's wife and explained how she helped him with his crimes trial. Cooper's wife purchased weapons illegally for him. One was a nine millimeter handgun. His wife used a driver's license with her maiden name and an old address. So the nine millimeter couldn't be traced back to her husband's car.

Carl's accomplices used their girlfriends in the same way.

The girlfriend was extremely cooperative. She was still interested and bringing closure to his case. And she gave us even more background on Carl Cooper and his associates. She told us about a third person who was working with them during the, the summer of 1997, committing robberies investigators placed Carl Cooper's alleged third man under surveillance.

He was a small time crack dealer.

If he in fact knew anything about the murders, his blatant criminal activity made him a liability to Cooper.

It's already as planned to arrest the dealer after a series of undercover drug buys and force him to come clean about the murder suspect. But it would take weeks, perhaps months to establish trust and purchase enough crack to charge him with felony drug trial.

If they arrested him before that the charges would not be stiff enough to leverage his cooperation.

Until then investigators had no evidence to arrest Carl Cooper for the coffee shop, triple homicide. And as time passed, Hoover would be more difficult to get to since he had insulated himself with so many.

By the end of July, 1998 over a year had passed since three employees at a Georgetown coffee shop had been shot to death. The FBI and DC Metro police believe that 29 year old Carl Cooper and at least one accomplished responsible. But investigators still had no direct proof to find it. They pursued Cooper from all directions, tracing his calls, watching his house and surveilling his associates.

Despite their relentlessness Cooper remained just out of reach. But investigators did learn that Cooper knew he was a suspect. According to FBI, special agent Brad Garrett, as you move into these cases further and further, and you talk to more and more people, particularly people in the street. They we're trying to get back to whoever you're looking at, if they're out on the street.

And it did. I mean, he knew in fairly short order that the police and the FBI were taking a look at him. The FBI and Metro DC police were not the only agencies investigating Cooper in nearby Prince George's County, Maryland. Sergeant Joseph McCann was investigating Cooper for the attempted murder of a police officer, Jim.

Joe McCann. The Sergeant was working with a female informant who also wanted to tell the FBI what she knew about Cooper. The informant end, Mr. Cooper had committed several armed robberies together, which is the reason why the informant was in jail for armed robbery at the time. So, uh, she knew him very well.

Thanks getaway driver. There's two others. Investigators interviewed her at a prison in Pennsylvania. No. She had no direct knowledge of the coffee shop murders. She knew firsthand how Cooper operated. The woman told about a pizzeria robbery that they'd committed in September, 1996. Cooper was the leader.

She was the driver of the stolen getaway car

Cooper's friend, the barber and the woman's boyfriend at the time were also in on the job. She said that Cooper carried two guns into the restaurant that night as he usually did.

His job was to shoot anyone who didn't obey orders.

Well, gunfire was needed that night.

They collected the cash drawer and wallets and made a fast getaway. Tell me just as best you can recall what you told the informant wasn't finished. She told the investigators about another robbery shortly after the pizzeria heist. When Cooper had fired his weapon that evening pooper carried a nine millimeter in a stolen 38 revolver. The barber drove the getaway car.

Their plan was to Rob couples parked in Avondale Park in Hyattsville, Maryland.

Cooper was unaware that the man he attacked was an off-duty Maryland officer

Cooper fired twice, getting him once. Eric, the informant said that Cooper had told her about it the next day, when the news revealed that the man he shot was an off-duty police officer. How long have you been? Fortunately, the officers survived the attack check. If police reports confirmed everything, the informant had said special agent Brad Garrett had every reason to believe her. Her level of detail was just phenomenal. You know, when she was able to, to lay out when it happened, where it happened with time, it happened, who participated even the interaction between the robbers and the victims that we knew about obviously through what the victims that told us during a robbery.

So she was really a pot of gold in this case. The information demonstrated that Cooper wasn't just a violent criminal. He was the leader of a band of robbers, informative, provided facts that the FBI could build a case around. She was basically the first bit of information that in my mind, and in the prosecutor's mind that really started fitting a Rico case or a racketeering case where you've got a group.

That's committing violent acts, interstate robbing commercial facilities, and that that we saw through her, the real possibility of putting together a federal Rico indictment that would include the coffee store. Triple murder. Building a racketeering case that proved Carl Cooper was the leader of a criminal organization.

It meant outlining those activities. In detail, the FBI secured a warrant to wiretap Cooper's phone. Now they could capture conversations, not just phone numbers, we're going to record any incoming conversations. Part of the warrant. They also cloned Cooper's pager number. Anytime someone paged Cooper, the agent's pager would also be.

Everything in place. Detective train he hope to stimulate conversation between Cooper and his associates. They began by inquiring on the whereabouts of the nine millimeter handgun purchased illegally by Cooper's wife. Well, we knew. That his wife had made that purchase of handgun for him in 1996. So what we did was we went out to the address that she had given the gun shop when she had purchased the gun.

And it turned out to be her mother's address as a ruse to get information. Yes. Investigators asked the mother, if her daughter still had the nine millimeter handgun. They told her they needed to complete a routine check of its serial number to verify whether it had been used in a crime. I have not disowned.

I just have not heard a woman claimed that she had not spoken to her daughter since they had had a disagreement some time ago. Investigators felt sure that she was lying. As we were walking back to the car, this a distance of less than 50 feet. Carl's pager starts going off with nine one, one 911 behind it.

And, uh, we knew that we had probably struck some kind of nerve there at that point already. She doesn't know where she is. I don't believe. Agents monitoring Cooper's home phone, heard the mother called a warn that authorities were looking for her daughter's gun.

Cooper's wife tried paging Carl, but he didn't respond.

She called her father panicking because he couldn't find the weapon and feared that she'd be implicated in her husband's crimes. If anybody's probably everywhere. Carl's wife was on a cordless phone sitting outside on the front porch and she's on the phone to one of her relatives, hysterically sobbing about how the police are gonna lock her up for this gun, that Carl's done something with this gun and that she looked in the hiding place in the house and the gun wasn't there.

So choral must have it. And she was just going on and on and on. So then she calls Carl. And he's on his way home. He's on a cell phone on his way home. And she says, Carl, I'm going to call this police officer right now. And he's screaming at her. No, no, don't don't call. I mean, just screaming at her on the phone.

After Cooper's wife hung up, investigators went to a residence to speak with her directly.

But no one came to the door.

Investigators were confident. They were closing in on the suspected murderer, but Cooper was not the sort of man to sit idly by. And allow himself to be cornered.

In September, 1998, metropolitan Washington, DC police, and the FBI continued to pursue Carl Cooper. The alleged ringleader of an armed gang wanted in the triple homicide of three Georgetown coffee shop employees, surveillance of Cooper's house, family and friends began to pay off for investigators.

Detective James, train him overheard an incriminating conversation between Cooper's wife and the girlfriend of one of Cooper's alleged accomplices. So she's trying to figure out why the police are looking at Carl and she starts what we call this guessing game. And she goes, was it for the shooting in the park?

Ms. He goes, no. Was it for the robbery? The pizza place. She goes, no. And then just, so what is it? And Missy goes something along the lines of, you know, the thing I told you about the thing in Georgetown and the other woman brings up, you mean the coffee shop and she goes, yeah, yeah. At that point we knew that his wife and this other woman had intimate knowledge of all these other crimes that Carl had committed $200 using her maiden name and mother's address.

Investigators were already aware that Cooper's wife had purchased a nine millimeter illegally for her husband. Now they would turn up the pressure on Carl's wife to reveal the whereabouts of that gun.

Investigators showed up at Cooper's wife's workplace unannounced to again, ask her where the nine millimeter was.

According to detective James training, they caught her completely off guard. Which was their intention to talk to you about the gun shooting sauce. It was like she hit a brick wall. I mean, just her face dropped. She became, she began to shake. She became very nervous and we're, you know, this very, very calm Mrs.

Cooper. We don't know why you're so upset. This is just a routine investigation. Okay. At home Hooper's wife told them that you still had the nine millimeter handgun, but it was in storage in Maryland. Good. She agreed to turn it over to them. Later that evening at her grandfather's house to the appointed time, FBI agents watched suspected murderer, Carl Cooper, removing what appeared to be a gun case from his house.

Agents were not sure what to expect at the meeting with his family.

Maybe it was a train just left in the car. He had the gun with him. The agent wore a wire to alert other agents parked close by if they should need assistance.

As they approached Cooper's wife's grandfather's Maryland home Cooper confronted them.

You accused the agents of harassing his wife, but he didn't prevent them from going inside her grandfather's child sat at the tables at gun. Since the nine millimeter handgun was already playing view, investigators were legally permitted to seize it. That type of weapon was not used in the coffee shop killings, but it was the same type used to shoot an off-duty officer in a Maryland park.

Sent the gun to the ballistics lab, or it was test fired and compared to the slugs removed from the wounded officer. Shallow grooves imprinted by the inside of the barrel on each of the slugs did not match, but the marks made by the weapons inject your pin on the shell casings matched those on the shell casings collected from the crime scene.

Experts determined that the barrel might've been switched or altered, but they agreed that this was definitely the gun used to shoot the officer in Maryland. According to Sergeant Joseph McCann. Once we received that ballistic report and we confirmed that this weapon that was registered to Carl Cooper's wife was used to shoot an off-duty Prince George's County police officer.

At that point, we had entered into a completely different realm in the investigation. Uh, it stepped it up considerably at that point. The investigators had evidence against Cooper for that crime. They had little to charge him for the Georgetown triple homicide or for federal racketeering to get to Cooper special agent Brad Garrett and his team turned back to one of Cooper's alleged accomplices, the crack dealer who had been under surveillance for months.

You set up multiple correct buys from this guy. Until eventually we got up to a quantity that he faced a mandatory minimum sentence in federal court. And then we arrested him. The key is, was to get him to help us investigators would pressure him to inform on Cooper in exchange for a reduction in his trafficking charges one, two, three to avoid years in prison.

The dealer agreed to wear a wire. He wasn't as close to Cooper as agents and hoped, but the dealer was close to another one of Cooper's alleged accomplices. Hey friend from the barbershop. Good, good. He called the barber to set up a wondering if I can meet you got the entire conversation I caught on tape.

Informant told the barber that police had stopped him on the street, asking questions about their involvement with Carl Cooper and the triple homicide that Barbara was already aware of the investigation and assured him that he had nothing to do with it. Barbershop guy kind of whispers to the drug dealer.

Look, I know Carl did it. He called me the night before and he wanted me to go along with him. But he never called me back. I said I would, but he never called me back. And then the next morning, bam, they were dead other than the anonymous caller that put them on the trail shortly after the crime. This was the FBI's first real connection between Cooper, his gang and the coffee shop homicides.

Now it was the Barbara's turned to be taken in agents hoped he would be the key to taking a triple murderer off the street. Yes,

a year and a half after a botched robbery and triple homicide in a Georgetown coffee shop. The FBI in Washington, Metro police were closing in on a gang of suspected thieves and murderers. Barbara believed to be one of them told an FBI informant that he had agreed to prop the coffee shop with ringleader Carl Cooper, the Cooper never called him back.

So the barber figured Cooper had committed the crime by himself, FBI special agent Brad Garrett decided it was time to question the barber directly and find out how much he knew about Cooper. So. We thought at that point. Well, the barbershop guy obviously know something about this, but he's basically saying he would have participated, but it wasn't called Sue didn't participate.

So we weren't, we weren't sure at that point then did Cooper do it alone. Did he pull somebody else in to help him do the robbery? We weren't really sure, but we then had enough that we could charge the barbershop guy.

He's followed the barber from his home in an isolated location.

Agents want it to be certain that no one, especially Carl knew that Cooper's suspected was being taken here.

The bottle was arrested without incident and transported to the FBI office for questioning.

The man, once again, denied any participation in the coffee shop homicides, but he did tell agents when Carl Cooper had said the night before the crime, he told us that Carl had come to him and said, you know, I've been surveilling, this, this, this coffee shop. It doesn't have any surveillance cameras. They take in a lot of money and I want to, I want to hit it.

And he said, okay, I'll go with you. What do you want Bob to maintain that Cooper never called him back to the beginning. And as far as he knew the ringleader had no other accomplices on the job. Even if the barber hadn't participated in the coffee shop murders authorities had enough to charge him with conspiracy to commit armed robbery, hoping for leniency.

He told them what he knew about Cooper until we get a car on May 1st, 1993, he and Cooper committed their first crime together. Barbara didn't have a gun, but Cooper said he would get one for him. They spotted an armed security guard at a DC apartment building. Cooper's snuck up on him.

When the guard tried to draw his weapon, Coopers shot him, then took the dead man's gun. Paul runs out, runs to him and they take off. So that's a murder. We didn't even know about the Cooper. Right? So that also was another case that was rolled into this. So. Rico diamond, we brand into the piece of store and it was a barber understood that stopping Cooper was the FBI's ultimate goal.

He agreed to wear a wire and meet. It was Cooper agents followed the barber through less populated roads after he picked up Cooper and his car.

The course of the recorded conversation. Cooper expressed his rage that the authorities were on his back.

He vowed to kill agent Garrett and detective trainer. So admitted that at one point he had seen Brad Garrett on the street and he had followed him for a while and he was laughing about how Brad didn't know that he was being followed. And so, um, it was a bit unnerving, but we knew that we had to arrest Carl pretty quickly.

Yeah. The authorities weren't going to take any chances. A few days later, they decided to arrest him for shooting the officer right in Maryland. They hope to search warrant for his house would provide the physical evidence needed to tie him directly to the coffee shop slang. Inside Cooper's home officers found ski masks, law enforcement clothing, and a variety of ammunition, but none of it could prove that Carl Cooper had murdered the SMI employees at the coffee shop.

The FBI's last hope was to sweat it out of him. Cooper knew that all they had was evidence of conspiracy and hearsay from secondary sources out really hurting the most. Despite two hours of grilling Cooper remained steadfast in his denial. That time had run out on the investigation.

We did not have a good case on him for the coffee shop murders. But if we charged them with the racketeering in DC, then we will be under a time constraint to get him indicted and convicted. And we just didn't want to place ourselves under that constraint. So we decided that PG County had the strongest case.

They were the ones that were going to be able to hold him without letting him get out of jail, this place. And all of our other people in jeopardy. After his interview in DC officers from Prince George's County, Maryland came to transport him to their jurisdiction. There. He would face charges of shooting the off duty police officer, but Cooper was preoccupied by the FBI's investigation.

He demanded to take a lie detector test to prove his innocence Cooper took one in Maryland, but failed miserably. That's when he finally broke. Well, it was as simple as that. I mean, I gave him everything that Carl felt that we had him in a box for the coffee shop murders and that he was going to be charged with those and that he was going to go down for those.

So he wanted to put his spin. I wanted to make, put him in the best light possible of course, with him being the only person who could he blame it on, but the victims and that's what he tried to do.

We're actually made three separate confessions each time taking more of the blame in his final confession. He claimed total responsibility for the coffee shop, killing.

He said he planned and carried out the robbery after spending time casing the shop, he called his, accomplished the barber, but then decided he could handle it on his own. Didn't want to lose the window of opportunity after the shop closed. And before the crew went home, he admitted to Sergeant Joseph McCann that he brought two weapons to the scene, which was his signature.

Carl Cooper's approach when you committed robberies was very business. Like it was a business to him. It was not personal. And if you did exactly, as he said, usually you would make it out of there. But on that night, three of Cooper's victims did not. And about nine 20 Katie Mahoney, Emory Evans and Aaron Goodrich were towards the end of their cleanup routine summary.

However, no. Why? When Cooper arrived at the shop, the door was unlocked. He ordered everyone into the back office with a safe go in the back, then move it back row. According to Cooper. The female manager tried to escape when he fired his warning shot into the ceiling. Cooper began to lose control of the situation and of his temper.

Cooper shot Katie. Four more times and left with nothing.

I think people were, were very surprised that one individual had committed this act, that it just, it, I think it's beyond most people's comprehension that that one person could go in where there's three employees and try to commit a robbery.

He said he rushed back home, laundered his clothes and disposed the weapons. They were never recovered in February, 2000 more than two years after the triple homicide, Carl Cooper confessed to and was convicted of 48 charges stemming from that crime, as well as the murder of a security guard, the shooting of the off-duty police officer, and the robbery of the pizzeria.

And leading a racketeering enterprise by pleading guilty Cooper, avoided the death penalty, serving a life sentence with no possibility of parole.

5 INDIANA KIDNAPPING OF ANITA WOOLDRIDGE

After several days of searching a former FBI profiler narrowed the suspect list agents and detectives followed the trail across state lines, hoping to find the victim before her time.

Drops of blood and a torn windows screen where all that was left to tell authorities what happened to a woman in Indiana. The 21 year old victim was snatched from her home on a bright spring morning. She appeared to have no real enemies. There was no clear motive.

This case was plagued by false leads and blind alleys. Each one using up valuable time as agents raced to find the victim.

In late spring, 1998, Howard County, Indiana, the rural Midwestern farming region was already enduring its first heat wave of the season. Those who weren't farmers stayed inside to avoid the heat?

21 year old Anita Wooldridge was one of them. Um, could you hold on for a second? Thanks. They have lunch with her grandparents and boyfriend before her afternoon shift at a shipping company. Her boyfriend was supposed to pick her up at around noon.

I have to go, but she would never make it.

At about 12:30, you need his mother returned home from work.

He was surprised to see her daughter's boyfriend standing out front. Needed his car was gone, but it was unlike her daughter to miss an appointment or to leave the garage door. My mother also noticed that the screen from the kitchen window that faced the garage had been removed.

Perhaps someone had broken into the house.

The front door was unlocked. Anita was nowhere to be found in the kitchen. Mrs. Wooldridge spotted blood on the kitchen table and floor. Oh my God.

Yes. She called nine one, one Howard County. Sheriff's did chief detective Steve Rogers responded to him. I don't know that any of us really knew exactly what we had at that time. We just knew that we had, uh, some very suspicious circumstances. We had what appeared to be, uh, uh, possibly a forced entry and that the screen had been removed.

And that's some blood indicated that there could have been a violent act. The detective yeah. Issued an APB for Anita and her blue sedan and called in a forensic team that included officers from the nearby city of Kokomo technicians recorded the scene while the evidence was stiff.

FBI retrieved blood from the kitchen, but could not determine if it was Anita's without a sample from a missing girl.

Scream found in the garage had been forced out from the kitchen window. Investigators dusted the area for prints.

None that were lifted, yielded any clues.

Detectives interviewed Anita's parents to learn more about their daughter. They described her as a responsible young woman who held a steady job and who would never break plans without calling. We had a missing person that was responsible and would not have just run off. We found nothing in our, um, Interviews with witnesses, uh, talking to family members that Anita had any problems at home that she would have just taken off without any explanation.

Okay. Good. The detective questioned Anita's boyfriend, who she had been dating for several months. I came over here. He claimed to have arrived at Anita's at about 1145. And had been there for 45 minutes when her mother pulled died, before that he had been with friends until around 11:45.

That left 90 minutes during which his activities could not be corroborated. He had no idea. And agreed to come to the station for further questioning if necessary, he's examined, it need his bedroom. Mrs. Wooldridge pointed out that it need his workloads were still there. She spoke to her daughter's supervisor, but he said Anita had not yet arrived to provide his name is Mr. Johnson, five one two three. The detective called again to see if she had ever shown up her employer.

Told us that, you know, she shows up when she's got a cold, she works when she's not feeling well, she's very dependable. And then fact that she didn't show up for work. That particular day was very significant. Mrs. Wooldridge said that the only thing missing from Anita's room was a red bathroom that she had recently embroidered for her daughter.

Forensic technicians, retrieved hair samples from Anita's brush to begin the lengthy process of mapping her DNA.

In the bathroom, Anita had left her glasses and contacts.

She couldn't drive without contact or still in her car. And her keys were gone.

Mr. And Mrs. Wooldridge had also discovered that their bed had been stripped of its comforter and the sheets were rumpled.

Investigators suspected that Anita may have been raped there.

Forensic technicians processed the room for any physical evidence.

Okay.

They examined the bid with ultraviolet light, searching for Seminole fluid on the sheets and blankets.

The bedding was clean in the garage. The detective found a wad of electrical. Take long strands of hair that resembled Anita's with tanks inside police suspected it he'd been wrapped around the victim's head, hold a gang. If that were true, it may have meant that Anita was taken from the house alive.

Detective spread out from the house, looking for witnesses. There was a neighborhood search conducted by talking to neighbors and walking areas and, um, see if she had been seen anywhere. Uh, and at the same time we were trying to develop any policy, any potential suspects.

Yeah. Uh, the deputy interviewed a neighbor who lived across the street from a world divorce. You remembered seeing someone in front of their house that morning, walk up to the door at about 10 30, the neighbor spotted a man carrying a blue backpack heading towards the front door. He saw no one else outside.

After he returned from his errand a half hour later, he couldn't remember if it needed his car was gone by then. Deputies were left with only hunches as to what had happened. He assumed that the worst could be, uh, an abduction, but we definitely knew we had a missing person. Um, so we just wanted to at least.

Uh, at the, at the very outset cover, the, all the basics of preserving the crime scene, um, obtaining any evidence that we possibly could, and then starting the next stage of the investigation, which would be doing as much background on the victim and trying to identify a suspect in, uh, in an abduction, if that's what's happened.

After 24 hours and dozens of interviews, no one had seen a Nita or car detectives interviewed a man who was a friend of Anita's father. Not really. He claimed that he had spoken to Anita on the phone the morning that she disappeared phone number that you had Paul Wooldridge, his records confirmed it.

Can you tell me about the phone call? The man said he called it about 10 30 or so. And asked to speak to Mr. Wooldridge. Hey, Anita said her father wasn't there and that she was the only one home before she could take a messy. She asked him to hold on. Someone was at the door.

Uh, Anita came back to the phone only to say she had to go. She did not say who would come to that. Increasingly detectives were convinced that Anita met with Falco, got to go. Did she say who was that? If this was a kidnapping investigators, suspected that whoever was responsible would make contact with a Wooldridge is.

Technicians tap the family's phone line. They would be ready if a call came in, investigators also began to search for anyone who might have had reason to harm a Nita, no immediate suspects. Other than we started looking into all those people that had been in contact with. Anita recently

detectives interviewed Anita's coworkers at the shipping company. They claimed Anita didn't have any problems with anyone at the jail.

But they did remember something a few weeks before she disappeared at a place where the employees often went to the lax. I need his coworkers saw a man approaching. It happened

he worked with him at the shipping company and it had several drinks before he started teasing the needle. Anita was polite, but clearly annoyed. Witnesses thought he didn't appear too happy that Anita had brushed him off.

I added that the man had not shown up for work the day that Anita disappeared, you can tell by the look on her face. She did not like it.

When detectives went to question the employee who was at home, parents of Anita. He claimed that his encounter with Anita and the restaurant was an innocent exchange. What friends were coworkers on the morning? She disappeared. You said he came into work before his shift and explained to his supervisor that he needed the day off.

Well, not me. I didn't want to do work on his car. His supervisor confirmed the alibi. Sorry for interrupting. As the hours ticked by family and friends posted missing persons flyers throughout the area. I can put one of these up and asked for anyone to call with information about their door, heartwarming car or the car.

You also contacted the media to spread the word beyond coconut Avenue,

air surveillance, and concerned citizens fanned out across the rural region to assist officers in their search. A lot of lanes and back roads are in the extreme portions of this County. We had volunteer groups, the, uh, um, civil defense, uh, actually went out and formed, uh, organized searches of wooded areas.

We felt that if we could find her vehicle, that that would give us some evidence to lead us in another direction, 48 hours after Anita had disappeared, detective Rogers received a promising tip from the mother of one of Anita's friends. The woman reported that Anita was having problems with another coworker at the shipping company.

Nita said that the man had sexually harassed her John

She was concerned enough to file a complaint against him.

Anita told the mother, if she wound up in a dumpster somewhere, you would know who did it. Investigators hope they could find it before it was too late.

They knew every hour she was gone lessen the likelihood Anita will be found alive.

Did he say anything after detectives returned to the shipping company? The supervisor told them that he had no record of a sexual harassment complaint filed against him. Yeah, he left two weeks. He left on his own opinion. He added that the man had resigned three weeks earlier and left the state for college.

Suspect remained on the list until detectives could determine his whereabouts at the time of Anita's disappearance

while the lead was being checked, investigators continued their search for suspects in the area. They asked to need his boyfriend to take a lie detector test. Since his alibi could not be corroborated on the morning. And Nita went missing the test consistent of only two questions. Did he have anything to do with the disappearance of Anita Wooldridge?

And did he know where a Nita could be found the answered? No. To both, but was found to be deceptive. He remained a suspect. The police had no evidence with which to hold him after two days of searching. Investigators were no closer to finding the missing woman and the chances that she was still alive, decreased with each passing day.

Two days after 21 year old and Nita Wooldridge disappeared from her suburban home in Indiana Howard County, Sheriff's had identified her coworker and her boyfriend as possible suspects in her abduction evidence found, founded her house suggested that she'd been taken alive. Investigators knew that time was against them.

Detective spoke to Anita's friends to find out more, most conveyed that they didn't know anyone who would want to hurt anybody, especially her boyfriend. Um, one friend would previously worked with Nita at a gym two years earlier said that Anita was nice to everyone, including difficult people. She recalled a member from the gym whose behavior towards the women, there was crass what's wrong.

His name was Victor steel.

They found him offensive, but he remained undetermined steel bothered Anita, in the same way.

Yeah, but she remained characteristically polite when she rejected him. According to detective Steve Rogers. What did I do? Anita was a personality that she was always very forgiving and willing to try to work with anyone. And that she had made an extra effort to try to get along with this. Um, the man's behavior never changed and his membership was eventually terminated.

I need his friend remembered that Victor steel lived in Howard County. At the time investigators checked on steel's background. His name came up, we were able to locate, uh, his name and the Indiana sex offender registry.

And learned from that, that he had been convicted and Monroe County, uh, I believe in 1984.

Of an abduction though, detective Rogers didn't know the steel had any contact with Anita. In the past two years, he believes steel was the most promising suspect. So far read this to substantiate his theory. The detective turned to retired, FBI profiler, Steve McVay for guidance. He had to three or four people that he had to look at as suspects.

He's wanting to see if we can narrow these down and to give some focus to the case. Uh, he has limited resources and certainly time was the most critical those, and if we could focus, then, uh, we'd be a little bit better off. The profile examined the crime scene reports and the backgrounds of each suspect 41 year old Victor steel's background stood out the circumstances surrounding steel's conviction.

15 years earlier had many similarities to Anita's disease.

in December of 1984, steel had stopped on an Indiana university campus where he was a student. One night, he waited outside for her boyfriend to leave like a niece. The young woman had previously turned down his advances

knowing she was alone steel approach. The house.

When the woman answered her door, steel pushed his way inside.

He pulled a knife from a blue backpack and threatened to kill her. If she did not submit to being raped, he'd had contact with her. Uh, he didn't live all that far from her. He carried the backpack that he had as same as in the first instance, which he used as a crime kit, where he brought his tape, his ropes and whatever else that he was going to use.

And that's very, very distinctive. After raping her. He forced her to walk with her at knife point. He told her to act like they were lovers or else he would stab her profile. Profiler recognize that part of steel's fantasy was to feel like he was her boyfriend. He had hoped to make this gal love him. His victim love him.

Uh, he didn't look at it as a rape. Now 15 years later, if it was for the same guy, he would have the same signature, but he would be more sophisticated about it. Most importantly, steel did not kill his victim. My God. He released her on the condition that she would not call the cops. She agreed then ran to the nearest phone to call 911.

Victor steel was arrested hours later, I think looks back on the case in 1984 as a mistake that he, uh, that he was not thorough enough in indoctrinating her or winning her over as, uh, as efficiently as he thought he had. And then when he let her go. She identified him and sending him to prison. Victor steel served eight years behind bars for first degree, rape and abduction.

He was distraught over the conviction in prisoner steel, attempted suicide twice. If he had a ducted, Anita, he was not going to make the same mistake. Again, Victor steel wanted to find a lady. That he could in effect make love him. And if he couldn't, if it didn't work, then he was prepared in my opinion to kill her.

And so love me or I'll kill you is a very succinct. A description of what went on in this case description, the profile is stressed, the importance of not revealing the investigation to steal. So Mike, Steve, what if the suspect felt police were onto him? He would probably kill Anita and himself, Kokomo city, detective Michael holes.

That hole was calling to work undercover and to help locate the suspect, the task of finding him involved as immediately in doing it. Uh, surveillance of his last known residence, which was the home of his mother, which was on the outskirts of our city here in Howard County, two and a half days after Anita disappeared, police set up outside the steel residence, no one was seen entering or leaving.

They needed a way to find out who was inside without blowing their cover. A car parked in front might be their way in. We observed that there was a vehicle for sale. Outside of his house. Uh, we seized on that as an opportunity to, to establish contact under a ruse of being interested in making the purchase of the car, recognizing that we wouldn't have to compromise our identity.

Posing as potential buyers, undercover officers wearing wires prepared to make contact with whoever was

no idea if steel or Anita were inside. Gotcha. The suspect might do anything to protect his freedom. Every moment's delay dwindled, the possibility that Anita remained alive.

In June of 1998, investigators searched for convicted rapist, Victor steel in the abduction of a missing Indiana woman, two and a half days after her disappearance, police set up surveillance outside his last known residence. Undercover detectives posing his used car buyers planned to make contact with the 41 year old suspect.

Each hour that passed decreased the victim's chances for survival Kokomo, city, detective Michael holes, Apple believed that there was still hope a sexual predator would enjoy a sense of self-assurance by way of his having made it from the scene with his captive victim. Um, That that probably presented a window of opportunity to, uh, to us as investigators that she was still be kept alive.

Wired for their own safety. They knew that approaching the house may put the victim at risk. If Victor steel discovered that he was a suspect, according to retired, FBI profilers, Steve McVay, I told him, tell your guys you've gotta be extremely discreet, uh, PA and this whole investigation, although we must press, because time is of the essence.

Uh, we have to do it in such a way that arouses absolutely zero suspicion on Victor's part. And if he had any suspicion whatsoever that, that he had come under suspicion of the police, then he would dispose of her. An older woman answered the door. She told the undercover detectives that the car for sale belonged to her son, Victor,

the detective said they were ready to buy now and were invited inside to discuss the price in the vehicle's history.

The mother claimed that his son had moved to Wisconsin a few weeks earlier without her permission or a warrant detectives were unable to search the house independently. They believed she was not likely involved, but they weren't convinced that she wouldn't alert her son to the search. He added that Victor hadn't hooked up his phone yet in Wisconsin.

So she had no way to reach him. No. You would have to speak with him before she could set a price. The detectives promised to keep in touch and look forward to speaking to the owner himself.

The FBI profiler remained confident. Victor steel was the primary suspect. We could not eliminate him. And in fact, the secure place that, uh, I thought he would have taken her to. And where he could spend a significant amount of time with her. It might very well be in a totally different area where no one knew him at all.

And no one would have any idea of looking for him there and that he very likely. They had gone and prepared a place and had in fact come back and taken her without his mother ever even elegant 24 hour surveillance by undercover officers continued as other team members, discreetly gathered more background on steel.

They learned he was unemployed and owned a red pickup, but they could not figure out where he was staying. With each passing day pressure to find the suspect and the victim mounted upon Howard County, chief, detective Steve Rogers. We wanted to find this young lady alive. People were looking at us and saying, well, gosh, can't you do something?

And we weren't at Liberty to talk about what we were doing and what we, what we thought we could get done. Uh, we had to be very guarded with that information. Victor steals credit card statements revealed that he had rented a truck in Indiana a few days before the crime company records showed that steel had traveled 910 miles round trip.

Investigators divided the distance in half and traced a 450 mile circle around Coca-Cola Indiana. Now that intersected was lacrosse, Wisconsin steals credit card records also showed that he purchased gas at a convenience store on the date. He ran truck

detectives called the parent company to determine the store's location. It was near lacrosse, Wisconsin.

They notified the FBI that it was likely Victor steel had crossed state lines with the victim. Yeah.

FBI special agent David Fitzgerald of the Eau Claire Wisconsin resident agency was assigned the case. We were able to offer them the ability to, to bring in other agents if need be to, uh, conduct investigation, um, anywhere within the state of Wisconsin. And if things were going to lead out of the state of Wisconsin, uh, the FBI is, is one of those agencies that has a network in place where we can contact people all over the country, uh, to help them out.

Six days after 21 year old, Anita Wooldridge disappeared for missing blue sedan was found close to her home. When a suburban street in Howard County, Indiana, it was just a few miles from steals. The car was unlocked. And the keys were still in the ignition

investigators, fear to need his body might be stashed in the trunk.

she was not there, but her red bathroom was. Underneath they found evidence that was more encouraging, severed, electrical ties. This was a very important thing with the profiler. He indicated to us that if these had been used to secure her arms or legs, that when they were cut from her, that would be to assist her in getting out of the vehicle.

There was a good possibility that she was at least alive when she was taken out of the trunk. Detectives found no blood seminal fluid or other signs of struggle in the vehicle, nor did they find fingerprints foreign to the car from the driver's side window, they were able to lift what they believed was an elbow print technicians, preserved it in the hopes it would match their suspect.

Detective Rogers asked the profile or whether they should allocate a portion of his limited resources to the search in lacrosse, Wisconsin. Steve Rogers asked me if, if I thought it was worth him taking a troop of his people, uh, to, uh, Wisconsin to look for. We even had the name of a town where a gas purchase had been made.

Now that was really iffy. Uh, in terms of that specific town being exactly where, uh, he had her, that part, I was not certain at all about, but we had nothing else at that point, a contingent of Indiana detectives headed for lacrosse, Wisconsin, where they believed steel had taken Anita. They met with special agent David Fitzgerald and lacrosse police at a command center in the city of 50,000.

They really didn't have any specific information that Victor was here and he was here now. Um, nor did they have any specific information that the victim Anita was here and was here now. Um, and they kind of looked at us and said, you guys must think we're crazy for being here, but, you know, they had been up for a day and a half and felt pretty strongly that something was going to happen in our area.

And we were just there to help them. Not wasting any time that evening investigators split up into several teams looking for steel's red pickup truck on the streets of lacrosse until four in the morning, without an address or even a general location of where Steeler this victim. The search was fruitless.

Once again, they turned to FBI profilers, Steve McVay, to help eliminate locations. They asked me whether they were looking for a life, a victim or a dead body. I replied that it was most likely. That she was still alive and would be as long as he thought he could control her and that, uh, and that he was not under suspicion by the police, uh, that he would keep her for a fairly significant amount of time.

He would keep her in a place that he had absolute control over and felt totally secure investigators, clung to hope that a week after her disappearance, Anita Wooldridge was still alive. Seven days after 21 year old Anita Wooldridge disappeared from her suburban Indiana home authorities believed it was possible that she was still alive.

They suspected convicted rapist, Victor steels holding her somewhere in lacrosse, Wisconsin, but chief detective Steve Rogers had no proof and no known address. We had a hope that she was alive. We did not know that she was alive. This was our last ditch effort, um, to, to find her, um, in the sense of finding her alive, that we had to get there, set up a command post and be ready for when we received the information where he could possibly be.

Remember to get it undercover. Detectives wearing hidden transmitters returned to steel's last known residence. His mother's home in Howard County, Indiana posing as interested buyers for the suspect's used car out front. Officer's hope to glean steals. Whereabouts from his mother Kokomo city, detective Michael holds Apple was aware of the danger.

Our concern was that if we were discovered making our inquiries regarding Victor steel at this stage of the investigation, that we might be contributing to the murder of this victim, that it might place her life at immediate risk. It was a risk. They had to take his mother maintained that she still didn't have a telephone number for her son in Wisconsin, which he did have an address.

The undercover officer repeated the address out loud to his partner. So it could be heard by detectives listening outside.

The immediately called chief detective Steve Rogers at the FBI office in lacrosse, Wisconsin at the, my team, people are in the street with the, uh, lacrosse, uh, police department and the lacrosse FBI. And I'm relaying this information. And, um, at that particular point, when I tell them, do you have a Clinton street in lacrosse?

And they looked at me rather strange and said, yes, I said, that's where he's at FBI and lacrosse. Detectives arrived in minutes. He identified the red pickup truck parked outside is Victor. Steve. As soon as Victor steals vehicle and residents were in fact under surveillance, I requested assistance with the local authorities there to go to a local court, a local magistrate and apply for a search warrant for the address on Clinton street.

And for Victor steel's vehicle and for the person of Victor steel, while they waited for the warrants, agents contacted the owner who lived close by to find out if steel had in fact rented the house, he confirmed the suspect was his tenant. Yeah, steel had claimed that he wanted to turn the building into a bookstore.

The landlord provided a sketch of the building's interior layout.

He also gave the FBI a key to the front door.

Yeah, outside the rental property investigators consulted the FBI profiler. They asked him what the chances were that steel was holding Anita inside the building profiler. Steve McVay warned that if she was there getting to her safely, it would be difficult. They were trying to determine whether they needed to.

Storm the place or whether that was even the place that he would have her or not. So I S I, I was confident he did. In fact, have her there, she would be very well secured. I did tell him that I thought there was at least a 50, 50 chance that should they attempt to storm the place while he's there, that he would kill himself and kill her too.

Investigators had no way to confirm who was inside. If they waited to go in, they might be too late. We were again, calculating with the resounding thump of this clock, ticking in the back of each of our minds and our hearts as to whether or not do we make an entry, do we wait? Do we stage a surveillance?

Watch and wait, do we go ahead and force an entry? That decision was in part made by us witnessing Victor, still leave the residence. After a week of searching investigators got their first glimpse of the suspect.

Climbed into his truck and drove away the surveillance team followed, but decided it would be imprudent to stop him for questioning. One of the risks that we did face and said, say he had a Anita at another location that was not the residence. And he decided that he did not want to cooperate with us.

And he just left. He may never go to that place again. And we may never find any of that. Agents trucks steel to a lumberyard

detective followed the suspect inside.

Steel seemed interested in long planks of wood.

I witnessed him make purchase of lumber. That in itself was a chilling observation and, and bit of information to convey back to the surveillance team, uh, because we had thoughts in mind. What's he using lumber for? To make it a cage to make a coffin

detective reported back to the other investigators.

They watched the steel returned to his pickup as a lumber.

Check it out.

Investigators continued their.

Steel Lee traced the movie take taken from his rental property. They had to decide soon if they were going to risk, stopping him without knowing for sure where he was going or where he had stashed Anita, if he had her alive and she was somewhere else, he would have went to her by now. But since he had not been.

Uh, away from the residence to any other location, we felt strongly that if she was alive, that she would still be there at that residence,

they decided they weren't going to let steel return to the rental property.

Take him down and pick up the cost of tech of radio to a uniformed officer. Just stop the pickup.

The decision would mean the difference between life and death or Anita Walker. Eight days after a 21 year old Indiana woman was abducted from her home, the FBI and local authorities stopped the prime suspect in lacrosse, Wisconsin. They believed Victor steel was holding a meta Wooldridge in a rented house nearby, but they had no proof that she was there or that she was still alive since they did not have enough to arrest the suspect.

Uh, lacrosse police cruiser pulled the pickup to the side of the road on the pretense of a routine traffic stop. The FBI approached special agent David Fitzgerald asked his suspect if he would assist in our investigation, he wasn't under arrest. And I, I didn't want to make them feel like he was, I had no probable cause that I was aware of at that time to arrest Mr.

Steele. And I just wanted a, to have a conversation with him. Steel agreed to go off and accompanied agents back to the FBI office. The sex offender claimed to know nothing about Anita Wooldridge, his disappearance, and lied about where he was living. Mr. Steve bill indicated that he thought that he had been stopped by law enforcement officers for his failure to register as a sex offender in the state of Wisconsin.

And he indicated that he had been in Wisconsin for a couple of days. Uh, and that he was staying in his truck at steel's rental property investigators prepared for entry. They would be ready when they got word. The one who signed by a judge. It was a difficult week. Detective Michael holes, the greatest anxious moments, uh, of the investigation.

I would describe occurred in a waiting the arrival physically of a search warrant that was being then prepared at our commands center. Uh, we had Victor steel. He was no present threat to anyone. We didn't know what the condition or circumstance, uh, Anita was suffering at that moment. They got to work.

The entry team use the key provided by the landlord. They exercise extreme caution, aware that that place may be booby-trapped

officer's swept through the rooms, including the basement, announcing it presence.

But the team heard no answer to their call cause a clear how's it glare. It appeared they had been wrong

at the FBI office across an agent. And detective continued their interview with Victor steel.

The suspect admitted that he wants, knew a woman named Anita from a health club, but he hadn't seen her for awhile. Without steel's cooperation, investigators realize they may never find a needle and they didn't have enough to place him under arrest. Again, Mr. Steele indicated that he couldn't help law enforcement officers.

Uh, he talked about the fact that he was, uh, not under arrest. He was detained and he basically said, do what you gotta do to get me out of here.

in the last rule authority spotted a large metal cabinet lying face up on the floor.

It's doors appear to be secured with a broken broom handle and a butter knife. We didn't communicate verbally at that particular time, but the communication was clear that we wanted to be cautious. Of booby traps. We wanted to be cautious about disturbing evidence, but we needed to open that cabinet.

Team members believed dead or alive. The search for Anita was at an end. They saw no suspicious devices attached to the box, nor did they hear movement from within.

Carefully. They freed. The cabinets handles

after the, he was alive. It was hard for me to believe that it was really going to be over. And they opened the box and there's like five or six police officers standing there. Like, thank God, take me home.

Anita Wooldridge told her rescuers that though she was not gangs. She had been conditioned by Victor steel, not to call out homie. He might make fake noises. So if I would scream for help, then he would kill me. And then when the police actually came to the door, I was still afraid to scream. Cause I thought he might be playing a tape or making it up.

She was handed over to the emergency medical technicians, except for dehydration. She remained healthy even after her long ordeal,

Dr. Steel was placed under arrest for kidnapping and sexual assault during questioning. And if you can't afford it, he remained unfazed. Victor really was not remorseful about what he had done. It, it appeared to me that if there was any remorse, it was in the fact that he had been caught. From the health club where I used to Nita had little to eat during her captivity.

She ate her first meal. She explained to investigators the events that began eight days earlier, Victor steel arrived at her home at about 10 30. She recognized him from the health club and invited him in. He told her he had been out riding a bike and asked if he could come in for a glass of water.

Didn't seem like a big deal that he came to the door. I knew he rode his bike everywhere. And I mean, it was really hot that day and I just never second thought it was going to get them a glass of water, send him on his way. Anita asked steel to wait while she wiped the blood from the kitchen floor where she had cut herself earlier, when her back was turned steel, drew a stun gun from his backpack.

I didn't know what was happening. It was also fast. And I recently go, I'm being attacked. And I started screaming, even though I knew. No, one's going to hear me. All the windows are shut and air conditioners are on. And then when he hit me in the stomach is just, I lost all control of my legs. Like they just went limp.

Steel disguised himself in women's clothes. Before he left the house, he first grabbed the bedspread than Anita's rope to cover her bound wrists. He tried to shove her out the kitchen window, but decided it was easier to walk her to the car. He locked her in the trunk. Before taking her to Wisconsin, he brought her to his mother's house and raped her.

I'd always thought I'd rather die than be raped. And, and then it was almost like survival mode took over my body. It was like, okay, we're going to get through this. And I'm going to do everything in my power, not to die like this and have my parents with unanswered questions. Understand me in lacrosse, Wisconsin steel shoulder, a metal wardrobe.

That would be a new home. He threatened to kill her. She tried to escape.

Anita agreed to try, but still didn't trust her. I'll take that forward. I'll beat you with it. He left a quarter on top of the wardrobe to indicate if she tried to get out.

I didn't like being confined like that, but at least if I was in there, I knew he couldn't touch me, but also made it very dreadful every time I heard the box open because I knew I was either going to have to play games with him or be raped or. Yeah, just see him

later. Returned home. Warm welcome.

Detective Michael Holzapfel was surprised. The case ended as well as having worked so many broken bodies. So many fractured stories. So many occasions that it didn't. It didn't come out. Like you would wish that you would hope, although this, this young woman suffered, uh, an incredibly, uh, uh, uh, devastating victimization,

she's still alive. And, uh, people work together to support her. And bringing her home alive.

Victor steel acted as his own attorney in his January, 1999 trial and was convicted of kidnapping, carjacking and weapons possession. He was sentenced to life without parole and serves his time in the United States penitentiary.

I think my goals in life are a little bit different. I never thought of doing anything in law enforcement. And now that's something I'm looking into that I like to do that to help other people. And, um, it just, it gives me a goal that, you know, I want other people like him off the streets. And so that's a little bit different than my original plan in life.

The life-changing experience would have shattered many others. But

Anita Wooldridge transcended her ordeal because of her strong personality and individual faith. She now hopes to become an FBI agent to help others as they helped her.

6 LOST BOYS

A series of crimes in a small farming community, left people kneeling in shock fear. It's the hunt for the suspects expanded. They turned to the FBI for help. They traveled over a thousand miles to find the deadly perpetrators before more innocent victims across their path.

in June of 1997. Hey, crime wave swept. I wear like a tornado. I left a trail of robbery, kidnapping, and murder, and it's awake. And then it moved on. No one knew where I'm Jim former head of the FBI's New York office. The FBI committed its resources to tracking down the suspects. By the time they were identified, they already had a 12 hour lead.

The pursuit would take the FBI across six States in their efforts to catch the killers.

June 11th, 1997, South central Iowa. The farming region, rich with crops and livestock began to stir as Dawn became morning. Most farm hands had arrived hours earlier to begin their chores. But one who never missed a shift without calling and failed to show that day, her boss and nearby farmer became worried when he called and got no answer.

Since she lived alone, he went to check on her

pickup truck wasn't there and the front door was a jar. Wow.

inside. He found the lifeless body of his farmhand. Barbara

Haskell County Sheriff's chief deputy called a Geest responded to the nine 11 alert,

20 years of law enforcement. I've been involved with about. The five or six homicides. So it's not something that happens a whole lot in Oskaloosa Iowa, where my Heska County, when we went into living room, we observed Barb Garber's body. She was setting upright, fully clothed in a chair. She was leaning over to the left side and there was, uh, uh, blood coming from her head.

The sheriff called specialists from the Iowa division of criminal investigation to process the scene.

aged woman had been shot four times at close range while she sat in the chair, admissions recovered 22 caliber shell casings, close to the victim feat. They found her half eaten breakfast.

The absence of defensive wounds on the body indicated the farmhand had put up no struggle. According to Iowa special agent Michael barrier, the house, uh, did not appear to have any forced entry. Um, it looked like, uh, someone had just entered the house either been led in or had, uh, gotten in without having to break in.

Um, the residents had a lived in look but was not ransacked and there was nothing obviously, uh, taken from the residence, uh, other than, um, Her her vehicle was missing from the driveway green pickup trucks. Um, I described the victim's vehicle as a late model, dark green pickup truck. And it was for personal detectives issued to be on the lookout for the missing truck to all law enforcement in the area

we're coming down. Investigators spoke to her closest neighbor who lived a quarter mile down the road. She had noticed something earlier that day when she was on her way to work in the pre-dawn hours, all the way down there she's on unfamiliar blue, hatchback, or stationed, Megan backing out of Mrs.

Garber's driveway,

but you didn't see who was inside and she didn't get the license plate. This vehicle was described as a older, not in very good shape station wagon type vehicle, uh, blue in color. Um, the vehicle was not a vehicle that had been seen at the Garber residence before, and it was not really associated with the Garber residence.

And so we felt that it may be, and probably was a suspect vehicle. As police were talking to the neighbor and alert came across the police radio.

Okay. I'll be in route a bank, five miles away in the Hamlet of Gibson had just been robbed

deputies from two counties responded

because deposits are insured by the federal government. The FBI was called Allen. Yes. The closest field office was 77 miles away in Cedar Rapids. Two males armed. Okay. All right. We'll be hitting right there. Larry. We got a bank robbery. Okay. All right. SBI special agent Scott French was assigned the case or they aren't worth it.

Right.

The small savings bank and Gibson just opened for business for the first time. That day to the town's population of 70. Yes,

it has one paved road to the community. A Gibson, the rest of the area is surrounded by farmland with a few gravel roads. Uh, leading away from the community. It would take agent French over an hour to get there.

Sheriff's deputies arrived first to secure the crime scene and take witness statements.

employees told investigators that the robbery occurred at about 10:00 AM. They had no customers at the time. And there was no guard on duty, only a teller, and the manager were inside when the robbery took place. All right, get your hands up. He was wearing dark ski masks, gloves and Brown coveralls burst into the bank.

No one held a shotgun while the other carried a handgun.

Yeah. Robert is scooped stacks of cash and bank notes into plastic trash bags. No up against the wall. Now they'd gotten away with $65,000 in cash,

though. They wore masks bank employees believe both men were white males. The Gibson savings bank did not have any security system that is no video cameras, no film to have recorded the robbery. This makes it difficult for investigators to have some evidence other than witness statements. Investigators found only one person who had seen anything a 10 year old girl.

You had to guess, what kind of car would you say? She told agents that she'd been riding her bike across the street on the robbery occurred.

you and ski masks. Holding bags had jumped out of a great car and had run into the bank. She wrote away before the men came out, the girl was either too young or too scared to get the license plate. Police put out an all points, bulletin the learning units to be on the lookout for a gray sedan as a possible getaway vehicle.

I felt the robbers in this particular case were from the immediate area. First of all, the Gibson bank is a very isolated location. Second of all, both individuals were wearing coveralls, which are somewhat indigenous to the working people in these communities.

Ten four. I got it. The deputy on his way to the robbery scene, headed for likely routes, the bandits would have used to escape.

Do you want me to check that that'll be the car matching the description two and a half miles from the bank. He noticed a gray sedan apparently abandoned in the middle of a farm field. No one was in sight. He checked the car and radioed in the license plate number. It was registered to a teenager by the name of Island Schultz who live nearby.

He thought it was extremely unusual that this vehicle would be setting where it was. And knowing that they were only just a couple of miles away. Uh, he drove to their house. IO communities are tight knit and the officer happened to know the Schultz family

at the teenagers home. He got no response.

The deputy found the front door unlocked.

Inside. He discovered 18 year old Island, Shults lying on the floor, shot to death. He radioed for assistance.

Maska County chief, deputy Paul DeGeest felt strongly that this second homicide was likely related to both the first murder and the bank heist.

Relatively sure. In our own minds that these were all connected, they were in a five mile radius of each other. And, uh, again, that's just not something you see a lot of in rural Iowa where you would have, uh, two bodies in a bank robbery all within a matter of, uh, two hours.

The recent high school graduate had been shot twice in the head from close range

and audio cassette and two 22 caliber shell casings. The same caliber found at the first murder scene were recovered, close to her body.

Like the earlier homicide investigators found no indication of forced entry and no defensive wounds on the young girl, Iowa special agent Michael barrier discovered another important connection to the first murder victim, Barb Garber, a neighborhood canvas in the area of the Schultz residence, uh, gave us information that a green pickup truck.

Newer, uh, in good shape was seen parked in the Schultz driveway at about 9:30 AM that morning. Um, that's interesting to us because, uh, Barb garbage pickup is a newer, uh, dark green Dodge pickup truck. And so we believe that, um, after her truck was stolen from her residence, that it ended up at the Schulz residence and that tied the two homicides together.

Both bodies were sent to the County medical examiner for autopsy analysis of the bullets confirmed what investigators had suspected. Each victim had been killed with the same weapon. A 22 caliber semiautomatic pistol, the FBI and local investigators assembled a command center in the Moscow County Sheriff's office.

They set up a hotline and contacted the media with a description of the farmhands Lake model, dark green pickup truck. We occupied a large debriefing room, which acted as a command post. We began to correlate leads that were coming in from all parts of the community. There was also significant media attention at this point, which increased the volume of phone calls that were coming in.

Deputies chased down dozens of leads. One was from a teenager who had seen a green truck that fit the description of the farmhands pickup. He was in the town of Oskaloosa in the late morning when he noticed the truck drive past with two men inside the witness, didn't see their faces and he didn't get the license plate.

Yeah, it wasn't much to go on since that particular truck was so common in the area, we received dozens upon dozens of sightings. Uh, most of which, uh, Turned out to be absolutely nothing. It was just a green, 1997 pickup. And everybody that was driving one at some point in time, that day in the Maska County area was stopped everyone except the driver of the murder victims, truck

investigators, fanned out to search the various small towns in the Haskell County for more promising witnesses. They found one who said he noticed something at around 10 30 or 11 on the morning of the crime spree.

you saw a dark green pickup truck near the town of Oskaloosa. The witness identified the driver as a local man whom he'd never seen in that truck.

he claimed there was a passenger inside with the truck pulled away before he could see who it was. The individual who reported it recognized the driver of that truck as being Jamie McMahon, a person that he knew and knew well enough to have recognized demon was positive that it was Jamie McMann. Uh, he also said that there was a second individual in the truck, but he could not get a close enough look to tell whether it was even a man or a woman, just that there was a second person in the truck.

What I want to do is I want you to take the background. At the end of the first day, investigators now had the name and face of a possible suspect in the two killings in bank robbery, 22 year old local Jamie McMann

agents and detectives hope they could catch up with him in his own identified accomplish before any more lives were lost. On June 12th, 1997. The day after two Iowa residents were killed and the bank was robbed, the FBI and local authorities had the name of a possible suspect. 22 year old, Jamie McMahon McMahon was last seen driving a green pickup that fit the description of the missing vehicle owned by one of the murdered women.

Investigators believed that an unidentified passenger traveling with him may be an accomplice. Special agent Michael barrier of the Iowa department of criminal investigation learned that Jimmy McMahon's last known address was at his parents' home in Oskaloosa Iowa. His parents were concerned to hear from agent barrier because they hadn't seen their son since the crimes that occurred.

We spoke to friends and family about Jamie McMann. We found that he had been, um, a good kid, hard worker, but then in the past few months, prior to these crimes, his personality had changed somewhat. They began to lose weight that he had stopped working, uh, and that it just appeared that he was having problems.

You mind, if I investigate is arrived at McMahon's home to search the house and find out more from his parents, this won't take long. Over the past several weeks, McMahon had been spending a lot of time with his 18 year old stepbrother. Christopher Kaufman Kaufman lived close by, but the two had different sets of friends and normally didn't see each other much

lately. They'd been inseparable. Now, both were missing. These are good because the bank had been robbed by two individuals. And because, um, uh, the witness had seen McMahon driving a truck with a second individual. We just had to assume that, uh, Chris Coplin was a second person with Jamie McMann. Detectives interviewed McMahon's friends who remembered seeing him with Christopher Coffman late on the night before the crimes driving an old blue station wagon.

One friend had lent McMahon the car for the past few months, since the suspect couldn't afford one. According to my Haskell County, Sheriff's chief deputy pulled the Geest. This vehicle was a blue station wagon, uh, which would appear to be a hatchback type vehicle. If you just drove past the back of it.

Uh, this would also tie in with the vehicle that the neighbors seen in Barb Garber's driveway. Earlier that morning,

investigators searched the car, but found no evidence that physically connected McMahon or Kaufman to Barbara Garber's murder. Any unusual behavior that man's friends mentioned that he had always wanted a dark green pickup like the victims, but the sticker price was out of his range. Jamie, he had an infatuation with, uh, this particular type of vehicle earlier that year.

He had one on order that fit, uh, the same as what Barb garbage was and did not have the money to pay for it. So he canceled the order. His friends added that the day before the murder McMahon had stopped by with Kauffman to borrow something else.

a 22 caliber semiautomatic handgun that he claimed he was going to use to shoot straight cats. The same type of gun was used in both murders.

Investigators asked his friends to call immediately. If the suspect contacted them for any reason,

authorities learned from several other friends that the suspected murderer had recently been abusing the drug methamphetamine, FBI special agent Scott French was concerned about McMahon's mental state since the illegal drug is an addictive stimulant. Abusers of methamphetamine suffer a variety of side effects.

One of which is they can be awake for several days. Second is they have loss of appetite, but of a greater concern to law enforcement is they have significantly clouded judgment. They become increasingly paranoid. And they may be easily agitated. Uh, widespread manhunt was launched for the stepbrothers and the dark green pickup truck that was still missing five 30.

The neighbor accounts reveal that a small blue car was seen in the garbage agents and police also notified additional law enforcement agencies and media outlets throughout the Midwest warrants for murder and unlawful flight to avoid prosecution were issued for McMahon and coffin. Initially, we felt that, uh, they had left the state and, uh, we could only speculate as to where, um, most of the investigators there felt very strongly that they were probably headed for Mexico.

Investigators, revisited the homes of the pairs, friends, and family figuring they would try to contact them with the recording device. McMahon's ex girlfriend gave the FBI permission to install a phone, tap and recorder. Figure out where he's at and give McMahon called agents would be ready to trace his location.

As the men hunt for McMahon and Kaufman continued a call came into the task force office. Two sets of local parents reported that their teenage daughters were missing the school. Cool girls, 16 and 17 had not been home since the previous evening. They were best friends and we're always together.

There's two killers on the loose. The parents feared for the girls. Life investigators discovered that McMahon and Kaufman had been partying with several girls at a motel in Oskaloosa the night before the crime spree.

at the motel. A clerk told investigators, the girls had stayed overnight and were still in the room on the morning of the crimes. Yeah, those are the ones

the employee saw McMahon and Kaufman with a green truck. Later on that same day, she said the two girls left with the stepbrothers.

Yeah, investigators issued another nationwide bulletin that the fugitives McMahon and Kaufman were last seen in Iowa traveling with two teenage girls. We were concerned for the safety of the girls. Um, I believed at the time that if, uh, Jamie McMahon was willing to kill someone, he knew. Uh, that the girls may be in danger.

Investigators responded to a promising tip that came into the hotline, but man and Kaufman had been spotted at a trailer several miles away from their family home. Investigators had no way of knowing if they were still on high, on methamphetamine, or if the teenage girls were still with them, not wanting to take any chances and not knowing their mental state.

Um, we had the FBI SWAT team command. Uh, basically we surrounded the, uh, the cabin and came in from several different directions, heavily armed agents, hope for the best, but we're prepared for the worst officers yells and McMahon and Kaufman to come out. There was no reply police teams stormed in ready to use deadly force.

In June of 1997, the FBI and Iowa investigators stormed a trailer in a remote field from the second day of a nationwide manhunt for 22 year old Jamie McMahon and his 18 year old stepbrother, Chris Coffman. The pair were suspected in two murders and robbing $65,000 from a bank. Two missing teenage girls were believed to be with them.

back here. Investigators found no trace of the future.

Sightings of the stepbrothers and a stolen green pickup were reported from as far South, as Texas to as far North, as Minnesota,

with $65,000 in cash and a 12 hour lead Iowa special agent Michael barrier realized the pair could be anywhere by now. We were unable to really come up with, um, any place that they may go. We had information that. They might've gotten to Minnesota. We also had information that they may have friends or relatives in Florida.

Um, but we, we didn't really have any solid direction of travel where they went.

after seven days of searching, the FBI got the call they'd been holding on for all over the place. Agents were ready with a phone tap. When Jamie McMahon called his ex-girlfriend. During the call McMahon asked if authorities had any idea who killed Mrs. Garber and Island Schultz. He was fishing for information.

He was trying to see what we knew and whether we even knew that they were suspects in the case. And she just told him, you know, what did you do? And, and, uh, why are they looking for you? And he became. Aware quite quickly that he was a suspect and that we did know that they were involved. Um, any hung up

the agent called a supervisor at the Maska County command center,

FBI special agent Scott, French learned McMahon had been on the phone long enough to trace his call.

after we received the phone call from McMann, I began the process of trying to track down the number from where he called. At some point we reached a snag with a phone company outside the area wherein they could not determine. Or provide the number until the following day agents learned that the suspected killer had cold from a hotel in Kissimmee, Florida.

The employee, nice photos of the two fugitives and confirm the two teenage girls were with them. I'll tell you when we registered here at this time, please

check out. But they had all just left. When did they leave? Yeah. So the phone company's delay had given McMahon and Kaufman just enough time to stay ahead of law enforcement, McMahon and carpenter the messed up. So they know we're looking for them. Now they know we're looking for agents were concerned that McMahon and Kaufman will be more difficult to find now, since they knew the FBI were on their truck.

All right. Well, thanks. And I'll, uh, get back on this. All right. Alrighty. Thank you, sir.

There were thirties had Ms. McMahon and Kaufman in Florida, the two teenage girls who had been traveling with the fugitives returned home safely to their parents take seat instigators questioned the girls about the time they spent with McMahon and Kaufman. The teenagers confirmed that they had stayed with a young man at the Oskaloosa motel on the night prior to the crimes.

The next morning McMahon and Kaufman came by in a green pickup with a lot of cash McMahon. The eldest of the group of 22 offered them a free trip to Florida. The impressionable teenage girls agreed to go with his stepbrothers and didn't ask a lot of questions.

Uh, the girls told us that they weren't aware that there had been a homicide and they weren't really aware that there had been a bank robbery as such. But they were aware that something had happened to allow, uh,

McMahon and coffee to have so much money.

The girls told investigators that on their way out of town, they stopped by the Des Moines river.

One of the stepbrothers threw a duffel bag into the water, but he never told them what was inside. After that, the four of them drove South toward Florida. For the first week of this trip with the McMahon and Kaufman, um, the girls treated it like it was a vacation. Uh, they were having a good time. They were eating out.

They were going to, uh, uh, amusement parks. One of their first stops was in Branson, Missouri. They're the four entertained themselves on carnival rides. The girls said, they took photos along the way. They played with them a couple of, uh, Instamatic cameras. And we took those cameras and had the film developed and we had, uh, photographs of McMahon and Kaufman.

And one picture in particular is of Chris Coffman sitting in bar garbage pickup truck. After that trip to Disney world, the girls said that McMahon and Kaufman finally confessed to them about the murders and the bank robbery.

Kaufman had dyed his hair blonde to disguise himself high on methamphetamine. The, our men also told the girls, they wouldn't mind killing them as well. The girls were frightened and told the fugitives they wanted to return home.

All right, look here, man. Gave him money for a taxi and train fare back home.

they told investigators. They had no idea where the stepbrothers were headed.

Well, they didn't say where they were going. They just gave us money and we left investigators, concluded the girls were not involved since they remained at the Oskaloosa motel. When the crimes that occurred,

they released the teenagers into their parents' custody without filing charges.

on the de Moines river and off duty Iowa trooper happened to come across a bang in the water.

he opened it to find a pair of black ski masks and Brown cupboards.

The officer also found a wallet with a driver's license. He contacted police and gave them the evidence,

the wallet and driver's license belong to the murdered Island. Schultz. The clothing matched with the robbers were wearing when they made off with $65,000 in cash from an Iowa bank. Jamie McMahon and Christopher Coffman remained the prime suspects and they were still out there armed and strung out on June 30th, 1997, 19 days after the search from a man and Kaufman began a call came into the Escambia County Sheriff's department in Florida.

the motorist in Pensacola wanted to talk to police.

you told him he was driving on a nearby highway when he noticed a green pickup. The night before he had seen a story about the man from McMahon and Kaufman on television, the truck seemed to fit the description of the fugitives vehicle. The motorist pulled alongside to get a closer look. He thought the driver looked exactly like the man featured on the show.

The truck also had Iowa tags.

The motorist pulled off and phoned police. The Escambia County Sheriff's department realized the motorist description of the truck matched the one Iowa authorities. No, not there Iowa authorities wanted to be sure this wasn't just another false. Yeah, it seemed pretty since the suspected murders were last seen in Florida.

They confirmed the license number and sent photos of the stepbrothers to the sheriffs in Pensacola

Iowa investigators alerted them to use caution since the fugitive pair were considered armed and dangerous. Okay.

urgent be on the lookout was issued for the green truck in the Pensacola area. Deputy searched, local roads, shopping centers and motel parking lots for any sign of the fugitives or the stolen green pickup truck

in the parking lot of a local motel, two officers spotted a green pickup truck. Motel residents usually park close to their room entrance, but this vehicle was obscured near the back behind a fence. It's Iowa license plate and description checked out. It was the murder victims, stolen truck from bio. She had no time to lose if they hope to bring in the fugitives before they alluded them.

Once again.

At Pensacola, Florida motel authorities had finally located the stolen pickup truck driven by Jamie McMahon and Christopher Coffman stepbrothers suspected of two murders and a bank robbery in Iowa, Escambia County deputies needed to confirm if the arm fugitives were staying there. Yes. The motel clerk recognized the photos of me, man, and coffee.

She added that there was a third man in their room. She gave deputies the room to her situation. Hostage situation. Police told her the motel had to be evacuated. Yes. Fearing that the stepbrothers had possibly taken a hostage deputies called in a hostage negotiating team killed two already Escambia County Sheriff's Sergeant Jerry Cox was in charge in this area.

They were armed. We knew that they were murder suspect. We knew they were bank robbers. Uh, they were seriously, uh, violent criminal individuals. So we got the call on our SWAT team and a crisis negotiators got to call out and, uh, and we responded to them. The motel, the motel was evacuated.

The hostage negotiating team set up an emergency center nearby SWAT teams took up positions near McMahon and conference room.

snipers set up on a nearby roof.

No one knew the situation with the third man or his relationship with the stepbrother. They had no way of knowing if they were all still inside. Negotiate a secure the line and attempted to get them on the phone.

from the man's tone of voice. The negotiator believed he was likely a hostage. When I made contact with the room, the first individual that I talked to was the hostage himself. He gave me a false name and I began to try to talk to him a little bit, knowing that was not the correct name, of course. And, uh, try to find out what his situation was, what his physical condition was and what the situation was in the room.

The man said he had just met the fugitives hitchhiking and stayed with them to party. Forgot. The step brothers had been awake for almost four days high on meth, and now they were finally crashing. There's no way they'll shoot. The man had since become aware they were murder suspects, that they were still armed.

Absolutely frightened out of his mind. He did not know what to do. And he knew that they were willing to take life. They had made statements to him that they would not be taken alive. And therefore he was afraid to make any moves because of what they might do to it. Bobby, the negotiator tried to convince him to leave the room with two other guys.

The rescue team would be at the door when he emerged while the men considered what to doing on. Look, man was meth all night.

Oh man. It's cops, man. You guys get you guys gotta let me out of here. One of my major concerns was the fact that they were known drug users and hadn't been partying for a number of days. Uh, When people are under the influence of drugs or alcohol, when it comes to negotiation, it's one of the things you have to be aware of is how those chemicals can alter a person's personality and alter their reactions.

Uh, they might be extremely aggressive due to their three week drug binge. It became clear to the negotiator that the fugitives were not thinking clearly, if at all, or how many. Well, we'll, we'll call it. His first concern was to get the third man out safely without more bloodshed it's already, as we're all too aware that the situation could turn violent quickly.

Paramount in my mind was, was the fact that if they killed two already and those, those, both those murders based on my information were coldblooded calculated murders with no thought given whatsoever to, to the consequences that they could easily do that again. Hold on, calm down. Just shut down down, man.

Just total. No man. Put that away. Put that away, man. Who is this shit?

Sharpshooters stood at the ready.

The negotiator tried to convince them to let the man out of the room before someone else was killed. You shouldn't have done that, man. There's no, no way. There's no way. All right. Fine. He don't mean nothing.

two hours. The armed men finally allowed him to leave.

SWAT members, spirited, the hostage out of the line of fire to where the negotiators continued to work.

did said he met the fugitives in new Orleans and had been with them for several days. You said they had a lot of drugs and a lot of cash in the room. By a couple of days, they only had one handgun. As far as he knew with two armed fugitives, still barricaded in the motel room. A peaceful resolution did not seem likely.

In June of 1997, hostage negotiators, and a SWAT team surrounded a Pensacola, Florida motel where two armed fugitives wanted for two murders in a bank. Heist in Iowa, remained barricaded inside their room, strung out on drugs, Escambia County Sheriff's Sergeant Jerry Cox was the lead negotiator. Yeah, it's the most difficult segment of the negotiations for me.

Was to try to overcome the emotional state that they were in as a result of their drug, use their prolonged, um, uh, activity of being awake for so long. Uh, and to try to. To direct them and a peaceful resolution. He spoke to 18 year old, Christopher Coffman. For some time, Chris, the young fugitive was aware that he was surrounded by police.

Sergeant Cox tried to convince him to do the sensible thing and come out unarmed. But one of the things I was able to learn from Kaufman was that he was tired, that he was just too, too physically and mentally exhausted to be making an awful lot of decisions. Worn out Kaufman passed the phone to his 22 year old stepbrother.

Jamie madman,

the negotiator notice the man seemed more lucid, more mature than his younger brother used it as a hook to separate the two. So I told him, I said, it's obvious to me that you're the one who's running the show in there. I need you to take charge and do something for me. And he said, what is that? And I said, well, what I need you to do is I need you to take care of your brother.

I need you to get him out of there. Well, the strategy worked, just go. I started this, let me finish. And I just want you to go, but the man didn't want his brother to suffer. Whatever consequences McMahon was going to face by staying in the room.

SWAT members secured Christopher cough. No only his stepbrother remained, but man teetered between indecision and despair. He knew his options were limited. The 22 year old began to weigh life in prison versus suicide. I heard what was, sounded to me like a weapon being charged.

It was an automatic pistol that he had in air. So it sound like somebody had slid the slide back and, and ejected a shell into the chamber, arming the weapon for firing. Gave me some concern. I pass that information on to our commanders and our SWAT team, but man's judgment was clouded you're there. He didn't want to spend the rest of his life behind bars.

Oh man. Confused and desperate. He looked to the negotiator for guidance. And the thing that seemed to work the most was constantly reminding him that as long as he was alive, he had a, he had some hope. He had a chance. Once he was dead, there was no chance. And that in Iowa, there was no death penalty. He had an awful lot of years ahead of him to figure this out.

McMahon relented to the negotiators insight

four hours after it had begun. The last fugitive walked out of the room on ours.

The negotiator was able to diffuse the situation without death or injury.

Agent secured and search the motel. They recovered $29,000 in cash. If the 65,000 that was stolen, they also found the 22 semiautomatic handgun on every table. Rested, empty beer bottles, marijuana and powdered methamphetamine. Ballistics tests later confirmed. The 22 was the weapon used to kill the two women in Iowa.

Authorities questioned the pair separately. I understand from your brother that you committed, both of them,

Kauffman told investigators. It was his stepbrother's idea to Rob the bank, to pull off the heist. They needed a car man already had his eye on the first victims, pickup truck, the truck he initially wanted to use as the getaway vehicle. I think I may have looked at a different print house. You might have to use your phone real quick.

Mrs. Garber knew McMahon and allowed the brothers into her house. Matt, just put the phone right back down. Please.

Shut up, sit down, shut down. Once inside claimed his step-brother egged him on to kill her. All right.

He wanted Mrs. Garber dead. So she wouldn't report the vehicle missing.

Often said he shot Barbara Garber twice then again, to make sure she was dead. Since McMahon loved her truck so much, he wanted to keep it in steel, a different vehicle to use in the robbery.

No man decided to try another friend of his Island. Schultz.

Like Mrs. Garber, their second victim led McMahon in, along with Kauffman parrot claimed they needed money for gas. She lent them $5 hour. As she bent over to put a music tape on Kauffman told investigators his stepbrothers shot her in the back of the head to make sure she was dead. That man shot her again between the eyes.

The stepbrothers took Schultz's car, keys and wallet over the next three weeks, the pair spent $36,000 on hotels, prostitutes or drugs before they were apprehended in Pensacola, Florida. No Iowa had no death penalty.

Jamie McMann, 22 and Christopher Coffman 18 faced the federal death penalty for two carjackings resulting in death.

They faced another federal charge for bank robbery. To avoid a death sentence. The stepbrothers pled guilty to all federal and state charges. Their convictions left many unanswered questions for the people of Iowa and my Haskell County, chief deputy Paul beast. These two guys were as common as any two boys next door.

I can't explain them why they would would go to this extent. To, to get a vehicle and, and to go on vacation or just to impress a couple of girls, it's just, it's just crazy. You'd never guessed that they would be the two type of individuals to do that. Knowing their parents, knowing their backgrounds. I mean, it just, just didn't make sense.

Jamie McMahon serves the rest of his life in Leavenworth, Kansas. Christopher Coffman serves his time in solitary confinement in the tough supermax federal prison in Florence, Colorado.

7 DEATH IN THE DELTA

In Memphis, Tennessee, a horrible crime terrified local residents. Most never heard the young mothers scream, but they felt the loss because local authorities searched for the perpetrator. They found many who had motive, investigators were forced to consider whether this was a random act of violence or a crime of deliberate calculation.

When a wealthy young woman was abducted in front of her in-laws home. The police had no shot at just suspects. The 25 year old victim left behind a tumultuous marriage and next husband and old boyfriends all around the FBI shot list. Um, Jim calcium from the head of the FBI's New York office, the suspects are interviewed the case grew no clearer.

To find the woman on her abductor investigators would have to first determine the motive.

Tunica County, Mississippi, just South of Memphis. Tennessee is America's third largest gambling destination

twenty-five year old, Shannon Sanders, and recently become one of the regulars on April 19th. It's 1996, the housewife from nearby Memphis, Tennessee visited her favorite cousin.

Shannon was having a good night. She managed to turn $500 into 5,000 with the high stakes blackjack team

at three 30. Am she cashed out and hit it? Sure. Test security. You ready? When players win big, most casinos provide a security escort to protect customers from theft. This casino is no exception upon Shannon's request a guard, followed her to the parking area. It was great. It was an hour's drive to Shannon's home in Memphis, through secluded roads.

She knew the route well, she loved to win, but could afford to lose.

less than a year earlier. She'd married her books, a multimillionaire who was 33 years or sooner

earlier that evening, she had dropped off her three young children from her previous marriage. At the home of their grandparents and Morse instrumentals,

it was about 4:45 AM. When Shannon pulled into the grandparent's driveway to pick up her children,

she needed to get them off to school on time in the morning,

inside the house. Shannon's former in-laws were awakened by a piercing scream, their former father-in-law rushed to the window to see Shannon struggling with someone in a basement. Okay.

Raised to assist her.

Neighbors also heard the commotion and witnessed the crime within seconds. The mother of three had been abducted less than 50 feet from the front door.

distraught grandfather called 911. Memphis police were immediately dispatched

and kidnapping medications that put response to mean the difference between the license

police arrived within minutes and interviewed Shannon's former father.

Memphis police, captain Richard, David Robinson Sergeant at the time recalls the, the shaken man did his best to recall what he had seen. Ex father-in-law heard a commotion and observed a car driving away. It's same time. Some other neighbors on the street heard the commotion and, and also looked out and saw a car.

Drive away and gave it a description of the driver and description of the car. Despite the dim light witnesses agreed that the driver had worn a red baseball cap. But their descriptions of the vehicle, very some described it vaguely as dark colored sports. Another witness was certain that it was a maroon Chevy Beretta.

None of them could describe the driver's face. Like I said that it was hard

on the driveway, close to the street. Police found two metal buttons assumed to have been torn from Shannon's clothing,

close by. They recovered a single artificial fingernail.

the victim's car was searched. The police found nothing to suggest the identity of her abductor or Shannon's whereabouts

her ex father-in-law had seen Shannon earlier that evening when she had dropped off her children.

He and his wife had agreed to babysit their grandchildren while Shannon celebrated her new husband's birthday at the casino. What's going on. Their former daughter-in-law had divorced their son less than a year before. Yeah. Still the relationship with her remained amicable and she visited regularly with the children.

Shannon's former father-in-law told police the name of the casino was Shannon and her new husband liked it. You know, confirmed she'd been there and won $5,000. But no one could say if she was with anyone in particular

news, that the mother of three was a duct just steps from where her children slept horrified local residents, according to Memphis district attorney, Jerry kitchen. She appeared to be a person who was very conscious about the upbringing of her children, because she had, uh, returned back to Memphis, uh, to pick her children up, to make sure that they got to school.

Memphis police questioned Shannon's ex husband, who was the father of her three children. Is anybody here with you after

He was at work when the abduction occurred in front of his parents' home, his relationship with Shannon had been stormy. They remained married for almost eight years. They finally divorced after Shannon fell in love with her present husband call her Memphis police were reluctant to eliminate and as a suspect, so early in the investigation, it Shannon's ex-husband's alibi was solid.

Who knows the reason why people get a divorce, but there's always got, I've never heard of a good divorce. She still made him pay alimony. Even though she was married to a wealthy person, join us, at least look to her present husband to learn more. Since he was a multimillionaire, they considered the possibility that Shannon may have been kidnapped for rents.

He owned a large security company here in Memphis. And he was well-known. Everybody wanted to help him because they knew him or knew of him and being that he was wealthy, she would be a prime target to be kidnapped for money. So far, he'd received no ransom call or letter thought. He'd been destruct since being woken at 5:00 AM with the news of his wife's abduction.

And regrettably, the last time they'd spoken that night, they'd had a fight it was his 58th birthday and his teenage daughters from a previous marriage had stopped by to celebrate happy birthday to you. Same evening, his wife, Shannon had planned to take him to the casino.

Hello? Hi, sweetie. After dropping off her children, she called to say that she was on the way to pick him up. He told her he wasn't ready. His daughters were there and he wanted to spend more time with them before going out tonight. No, Shannon became angry. According to her husband, she felt he was putting his children ahead of their plans.

He told her he could be ready in a half hour, but she hung up on him. Hello. You expected that you'd cooled down and pick him up. But when he tried to call later, she did not answer. She, she, and I would just sit down, I guess there's just such a difference. Elise asked if he knew anyone who might want to harm Shannon.

The last thing I said, she said, the husband, you mentioned an ex-boyfriend against whom Shannon had filed charges of harassment earlier.

He believes the ex-boyfriend drove a Chevy Beretta

headquarters. Police checked with DMV, but found no records that her ex-boyfriend or any of his family owned a Beretta. The criminal background check did confirm that a judge had ordered her ex lover to have no contact with Shannon over the past year.

investigators went to question Shannon's ex-boyfriend, but he was not at home more. Had he shown up for work.

Your sister lived in the same neighborhood, a few blocks from where Shannon had been abducted.

She reported that she had seen a suspicious car drive past her house on the night of the crime. She was out on the porch around the time of the abduction. When I'm a room Chevy Beretta sped by heading out of the Navy.

She said she didn't recognize the driver. At first, when she saw a photo of Shannon's wealthy husband in a news report, she was sure it was him.

Don't Memphis police at first considered the possibility that Shannon had been abducted for ransom. They now began to consider another possibility. I always, in the back of your mind, do the, her being married to wealthy person and. The difference in our ages that, uh, something could have happened to her to get rid of her.

Um, there was, we just didn't know. So we tried to cover every angle that we could. Memphis police asked Shannon's husband to provide a formal statement with his lawyer present. He filled in detectives about his relationship with Shannon.

Police knew that he had met Shannon while she was still married, working at the security company.

She worked for him, but soon their relationship took a personal term.

Their romance led to marriage, but the magic didn't last, nothing else that you can think of. Nine months later, they began negotiating a post-nuptial agreement, outlining terms in the event that troubled union in Brook, both had previous marriages that ended in divorce and Shannon needed to feel certain that she would retain custody of her children.

They'd filed it just 10 days before Shannon's abduction, fingerling, sufficiently. Well to come to. Shannon's husband emphasized that it was his wife who wanted the agreement. He claimed money was not the issue since they kept separate banking.

Do realize that when police asked the husband agreed to reinforce his statement with a polygraph.

To cover all possibilities. Police checked local morgues, jails and hospitals, but after a week, investigators had no solid leads to Shannon's. Whereabouts.

Police in Memphis received dozens of calls from local residents, most were well-intentioned but unproductive. And your name again, all had to be checked. A woman named Sharon Powers in nearby Clarksdale, Mississippi 80 miles South of Memphis. Abduction was reported in the paper and on the news and description of the car was given, she had contacted the Memphis police department saying that she thought that maybe her husband had was in bind, uh, because of description of the car.

She told Mississippi police that she believed her husband Lee may fit the suspect description. The day after the crime was reported, he had worn a red cap and left town in their red Chevy Beretta to see his mother,

woman said that she and her husband had been fighting. Police asked her to have him call when he returned. They weren't optimistic. The reports sounded like a possible domestic dispute, unrelated to the case.

On May 3rd, 1996, police responded to another call from a concerned citizen, trying to help. At a casino in Tunica County, Mississippi, the witness believed he had spotted Shannon Sanderson dressed as a casino employee.

I'm sorry. An officer approached her. He realized that it was a case of mistaken identity. It was one more call among hundreds of false leads that frustrated the investigation.

After two weeks of searching. Local investigators were no closer to finding the missing mother.

Her family was left only with the hope that she was still alive

in the spring of 1996. Memphis police continued their search for twenty-five year old. Shannon Sanders would have been abducted from the front of her former in-laws home.

instigators had questioned her wealthy husband past lovers and area residents, but none offered clues to her. Whereabouts

any investigation? Authorities, try first to eliminate those people closest to the victim. After more than two weeks of searching Memphis police, captain Richard, David Rolson feared. The time was running out. Dude our past boyfriends and lovers, we just didn't know what happened. But as the days went by the chances of finding her life or slimmer and slimmer on May 6th, Shannon's ex-boyfriend finally came in for questioning.

He had only recently completed his year long probation of harassment charges against Shannon. He claimed to be asleep in his mother's house at the time of her abduction, according to the ex-boyfriend, he avoided Shannon is his probation required, but Shannon continued to call him complaining that she wasn't happy with her new marriage.

He added that he would have to talk to his lawyer before agreeing to take a polygraph.

He remained a potential suspect. But as with Shannon's husband, no hard evidence existed to prove nor disprove is involved. Then on May 9th, 1996, 40 miles South, from where Shannon had been abducted Sheriff's in DeSoto County, Mississippi caught a land in the town of Eudora.

two people had been inspecting their new property. And when they noticed a strong odor

then they discovered a woman's decomposing body. The DeSoto County crime scene technicians set up a grid around the immediate area item. They conducted a line search looking for anything that might be a clue. They labeled and recorded every item they came across. As they drew closer to the body, 15 feet away, they found a woman's high-heeled shoe.

closer to the body. They marked the location of another DeSoto sheriffs check their records, but found no women reported missing locally. They broadened their search to include larger towns and cities in the region. When they contacted Memphis authorities. Police there told them that a 25 year old mother of three named Shannon Sanders and had been missing for more than two weeks.

Deputies learned that she was blind, approximately five, five, 130 pounds at a small tattoo and was last seen wearing a dress high heels, a jacket with metal buttons and pink artificial fingernails.

that description fit the body, but they needed an autopsy to confirm her identity and cause of death. Sorry. The medical examiner determined that the victim had been killed by a single 25 caliber bullet to the right template. Yes, sir.

The victim's clothes were removed and preserved to check for trace evidence that might lead to the killing

the body dead. And estimated two to three weeks was to decompose to recognize that over her left breast examiners found a small tattoo. That was still visible.

It said, I love you. Robert Shannon Sanders had such a tattoo.

The medical examiner compared her dental records to x-rays from the body. They confirmed the ID. This was Shannon Sanderson's body. The abduction was now officially a homicide in Memphis assistant district attorney Jerry kitchen was called in his first task would be to somehow narrow the suspect list the police had developed over the past three weeks.

It's somewhat unusual in that we have relatively few murder cases that we would classify as mystery homicides, where, uh, someone's not. Either developed as a suspect rather quickly or arrested, uh, soon after the incident. Um, but in this particular case, uh, it was a mystery, uh, homicide with numerous suspects that, uh, were listed as potentially being involved in the abduction and killing of the victim.

The assistant district attorney first called the Tennessee Bureau of investigation to conduct polygraph examinations to help eliminate potential suspects. He also contacted the FBI since Shannon's body was found across the Tennessee state line

supervisory, special agent, Jennifer Achin from the FBI's Memphis field office was assigned as case agent. They felt they needed some additional resources. The case was a very difficult case across jurisdictions and they wanted the FBI to be involved as part of the team, um, working towards a solution.

Cause it was, it was not an easy, an easy case. Emphasis is hope that agent Akins experience would help unravel the complexities of this case. Local residents were fearful that Shannon's killer is still out there not knowing if or when he would strike it

in the spring of 1996. The body of 20 five-year-old Shannon Sanderson and mother of three was found in Eudora, Mississippi 40 miles from our Memphis, Tennessee, the FBI together with state and local investigators needed to shorten the lengthy suspect list that included Shannon's husband and past lover,

assistant district attorney, Jerry kitchen, hope polygraph examinations could help focus their search. This investigation was difficult in that there were a lot of suspects in this particular case throughout the victim, it was live. She had, of course been divorced and naturally in any type of murder case.

So you, some, you, you do focus in and you do look at, uh, relatives or acquaintances or husbands, uh, any type of relationship that the victim may have been involved in that, uh, uh, could. Uh, lead back to some type of dispute or domestic violence, Tennessee state authorities tested several of Shannon's ex lovers.

They asked them their whereabouts on the night of the abduction. They asked directly if he had abducted or killed Shannon, all denied any involvement. The tests revealed no deception.

Investigators corroborated their alibis and eliminated them as potential suspects.

They also polygraph the witness who claimed to have seen Shannon's current husband driving a maroon Chevy Beretta in the neighborhood moments before the abduction occurred, it was the same type of vehicle. Other witnesses have described that Shannon was forced into. But the woman was found to be deceptive

though. Police now believed her claim was false, that she had seen Shannon's husband driving the getaway vehicle. They also knew that Shannon's brief marriage with her wealthy husband had been Rocky. They wanted to confirm once. And for all that, he had not been involved in any way. There's a question about honesty and what this crime occurred at four o'clock in the morning.

The victim's husband had indicated that he went to bed and that there was no one else that he was with. And so he really had no alibi. And so that was an area that was difficult for us to get over, uh, because we could not lock down exactly where he was and what he was doing without, uh, other than what he was telling us.

Investigators contacted Shannon's husband to be polygraphed as though he had previously agreed to do so on advice from his lawyer, he declined

heart medication that he was taking may have induced a false reading according to his lawyer. Are you feeling any objections for captain Rolson your husband's refusal? Didn't alleviate the suspicions that surrounded him. You couldn't understand if he didn't have anything to do with it, why he wouldn't be wanting to cooperate and being a homicide detective you're suspicious and, and.

Uh, it just made him more suspicious in terms of incriminating evidence investigation was at a standard

revisory special agent, Jennifer Achin, hope to refocus the investigation by examining leads that may have been overlooked. We have to look at all of the POS and, and that's, you know, part of the battle in the beginning is not to get too far down the road in speculating about what kind of, of guide this could be.

Um, and, and what, you know, what his relationship or non-relationship would be to the victim. What we did then is identify what else, what other possibilities. Um, do we still need to explore

one possibility though? Not a promising one was Sharon Powers who earlier reported that her husband may have matched the vague description of the suspect. He gets more information about. But now she wasn't so sure about that previous claim.

She told police she had overreacted, reinforcing their beliefs, that she'd only been trying to get back at her husband for leaving her. She said that her husband had left town, that they had had some, you know, marital disputes. They felt that perhaps, um, this report was really just sort of sour grapes and that she was trying to get her husband, um, maybe a strange husband into trouble of some kind of really just simply did not know how much wait to give, uh, this rather conflicted.

kind of half-hearted story that she was telling, but her husband wasn't a serious suspect. Police wanted to talk with him, but bulletin for Gerald Lee powers was issued that he was wanted for questioning in Tennessee. FBI agents and Tennessee investigators met to review the casino surveillance tape of the blackjack table, where Shannon had won the now missing $5,000.

Her growing pile of chips would certainly make her an attractive,

they viewed the tape to see if a stalker could be seen.

If that was the killer's intention. Agent Aiken questioned why he would wait so long to make his move. Clearly she had been winning for a while. She was there late at night. There were a number of factors that made her visit to that casino, rather high risk. And yet we had this abduction occurring almost an hour to an hour and a half after she left that environment.

So first we had to determine, did it have anything or nothing to do with her visit to that casino? The tape showed Shannon. It was inadequate to reveal whether she was being stalked. Investigators were no closer to finding the truth as they kind of plated what to do. Next investigation veered in an unexpected direction.

On May 22nd, 1996 near Hebbronville Texas 750 miles from where Shannon was seen, forced into a car described as a Chevy Beretta, the vehicle fitting that description there radically swerved away from a border checkpoint. The vehicle had Mississippi plates. One of the patrol guards raced after three, even the driver to be a potential border or smell

in may of 1996. As the investigation continued into the kidnapping and murder of a young Tennessee mother, us border patrol agents, chase down a fleeing maroon Chevy Beretta with Mississippi plates, the type of car described by witnesses in the abduction.

Corn at a dead end, the suspect loses, drop it, drop it up against the car, up against a cop. Then back down and confronted by the agents gun.

He had 14, $100 bills in his pocket. The driver said his name was Gerald Lee powers, but held no driver's license

cursory search of the car revealed no illegal drugs or anything.

in the trunk. Border agents recovered a stolen weapon, registered in Arkansas. The car was locked and remained in that spot. Under armed guard until FBI agents could conduct a more thorough search

agent. Evan Ray from the FBI field office in the radio, Texas was contacted since assaulting a border patrol officer is a federal offense

agent Ray confirmed the identity of the driver. When he learned the Gerald Lee powers had been involved in another altercation at the Mexican border. Uh, I spoke to us customer service officials who had indicated that they had had an incident that day as well, in which an individual had fled and had left several pieces of identification behind on the counter when they fled.

And so we were then in possession of, uh, several pieces of identification of Mr. Power, uh, license plate check revealed that the vehicle was registered to his wife, Sharon and Clarksdale, Mississippi. Agent Ray also discovered the Gerald leap powers at a violent past and was currently wanted for questioning in the abduction and murder of Shannon Sanderson.

after contacting Memphis authorities, he traveled to Hebbronville to process power's car on site,

the Chevy Beretta matched the vehicle witnesses have described as the abduction.

Agents hope something inside, but link the vehicle and powers to the murder of Shannon centers.

A sheet and pillow case along with the trunk liner were bundled into evidence bags. Let's tape this stuff up, we'll get it back to headquarters.

When you're retrieving evidence like that, you have no idea what the results of the laboratory examinations are going to be in the end. You just try to get the best, uh, and the most evidence that you can and let the lab do.

Their job agents were less hopeful. They'd find something in the cars interior, since it appeared to have been recently clean vacuum.

Hundreds of miles from the nearest evidence response team, agent Ray improvised with the tools he had at hand. One item that we needed to search for were Harrison fibers in the back seat area. We didn't have the specialized equipment that the evidence response team would have. And so I used an unopened lint roller that I had.

At the office of the type one might use on a, on a suit to, as an adhesive lift initially obscured by the front seat, the agent found a pink artificial fingernail on the floor. It was similar to those. The victim had worn at the time of her abduction, Memphis prosecutor, Jerry kitchen believes this could be the clue that could definitely play Shannon Sanders and empowers.

ADRA had called us and told us that he is found a fingernail in the back seat area of the, uh, flow board of this vehicle, which is where we had felt that based upon the witnesses, uh, uh, information they had given us that, that the victim had been placed in the back seat. Of the vehicle that took her away.

Memphis authorities came to Laredo to question Gerald Lee powers

powers told them that he knew nothing more than what he'd heard on the news. He admitted to being at the casino that night, but it left early to check on his terminally ill neighbor. And while the interview continued, investigators spoke to his neighbor in Clarksdale, Mississippi who denied that powers had been there at that time.

Weren't 100% convinced Gerald Powers was our suspect. We just felt it was kind of suspicious that he was, he was trying to give a false alibi and that of course, The neighbor was very ill and could have been mistaken because he had been there at different times. Investigators hope that powers wife, Sharon might be able to corroborate the neighbor's statement.

She had initially told police her husband fit the description of the suspect who witnesses glimpse to the abduction. A man who wore a red baseball cap. Now she added that he made frequent trips to the casino with a victim and spent her

still. She did not. No. If he had visited their neighbor that night and denied that her husband had anything to do with the abduction and murder of Shannon Sanders. Yeah. Investigators feared. They might just be wasting their time, but FBI special agent Jennifer Achin. Wasn't so sure. We sensed her ambivalence.

We knew that she, you know, had come forward even with her kind of. Half-hearted story. We knew she'd come forward for a reason and that there was more, she needed to tell second Slater, Gerald Lee, Pam agent akin realized that you would need to invest a great deal of time to develop the trust of Sharon Powers.

That's tremendous. As the dialogue with Sharon Powers continued over several weeks. The FBI contacted Tom Scott director of surveillance at the casino where the victim had gambled prior to her abduction. Scott was asked to confirm if Gerald Lee powers had been, did that same night on any of the 600 cameras and the 95,000 square foot casino.

Jennifer akin from the FBI gave us a, uh, a basic description of what the suspect possibly was wearing on the night in question. Um, and that's what we went with with as a general description from color shoes, to jeans, to a certain type jacket and possibly a ball cap any given day, uh, you can have approximately 3000 to 10,000 people within a casino.

Scott and his team searched hundreds of hours of footage looking for a man in a red baseball cap and yellow shirt. Their main focus was the blackjack table where Shannon spent most of the night. If the suspect was stationary, it's pretty easy. But, uh, in a casino it's quite an exciting place to be in and everybody kind of wanders around and they go to slot machine, a slot machine or restaurants or table games.

We could not locate the individual investigators. Look to Sharon Powers for more detail about her husband's activities that night they did what they could to make her feel comfortable. Don't worry. One of her neighbors and police officers provided her with reassurance and support. She was a woman torn between her empathy for the victim and her feelings towards her husband.

She was in love with this man. I think it was difficult for Sharon. To accept the fact that the victim had been a mother of three young children. Um, she herself was a mother of three children and, uh, I'm very much related, uh, to the victim. Slowly Sharon Powers worked through her internal conflict.

She began to open up revealing what our home life was like with her husband, Gerald Lee powers. She said he, the house, there were three kids from previous marriages were afraid of him. Sharon admitted that she was too, he kept a bell in his chair when he rang, Sharon came up, despite his controlling tackle, her feelings for him were deep.

This is a woman who had. Really kind of lived under the thumb of, uh, Gerald Lee powers for a number of years. I believe by then they had been married four or five years. And, uh, she, um, I don't want to say liked it that way, but that was what she was used to. That was familiar. Um, it was not, uh, it was not familiar to her to be braking.

With him to be disloyal. Despite her fear, Sharon continued to open up to investigate on April 19th. The day Shannon Sanderson was abducted. Gerald came home, shut up and sit down. Sharon was angry because she thought he'd spent the night with them. What's on your shirt. Don't worry.

She noticed blood on his shirt and a cut on his arm.

He claimed he'd fallen down at a casino. He'd been visiting. Do you remember what color the shirt was? Sharon didn't believe what he told her, but she didn't press it. No Sharon refused to say anymore. And neither would her husband, without something stronger prosecutor, Jerry kitchen would be unable to press charges on Gerald Lee powers.

We still didn't have anything concrete that. He had been involved and it was just, uh, instinct. Uh, I think that was leading us at this point that he was our man, but at the time we did not have the results back from the lab. Investigators hope the FBI would reinforce their hunch, that Gerald Lee powers was responsible for leaving Shannon Sanderson's children.

Motherless.

In the summer of 1996 after Gerald Reed powers was indicted for assaulting a border patrol officer in Texas, the FBI and Memphis investigators suspected he was also responsible for the murder of it. 25 year old mother of three, lacking physical evidence. Memphis prosecutor, Jerry kitchen was unable to charge powers for his involvement.

Or to know for certain, if one of the victim's former lovers had hired him to commit the crime, there was always that possibility, um, the way she was killed in the manner in which she was abducted, that it appeared like it wasn't just something random that it had been something planned, all the other suspects that appeared to have a motive or possibly, uh, uh, emotional reasons why someone would, would want to have someone killed.

Jealousy or rage or, uh, other, uh, factors, investigators hope the suspect's wife, Sharon Powers could tell them more. The reluctant at first, after many meetings over several weeks, Sharon grew more comfortable. She finally opened up to FBI special agent Jennifer Achin. When she finally told the story and in its entirety, um, what we heard was really a chilling tale.

Of of his stalking of the victim and to end the abduction of the victim and then taking her to this rural area and, uh, and robbing her of, of not only the $5,000 that she had won that night, but also of, of the jewelry that she was wearing. Sharon story was strong, but without corroborating evidence, it would not be enough to convict, to even indict Jill powers for murder.

Trying to help. She told investigators that her husband had thrown the murder weapon, a handgun into an abandoned canal near the casino in Mississippi, Memphis police, captain Richard Rolson accompanied local divers to help search for the Sheriff's department divers dove into this hole and crawled inch by inch.

Searching for this pistol. We never did locate it. And then that's when Ms. Powers told us that he had thrown it into the river, which was about a hundred yards away. The current at that location was too Swift for anybody to dive in the Mississippi river. It left investigators with more doubt and no corroboration that Sharon Powers was telling them the truth.

The suspect's wife also told him about a school bus driver from Mississippi who her husband believed, had seen him close to where he dumped Shannon's body. Did you happen to notice the driver. Police tracked down the driver who confirmed Sharon story

at 7:00 AM. About two hours after Shannon Sanderson had been abducted. The driver noticed a maroon Chevy Beretta backing down the dirt roadway of the vacant property, where the victim's body was later.

The bus driver remembered it because the property has been vacant for so long. Um, But the driver didn't see who was in the car and didn't get the license plate

searching for further corroboration investigators turned to Tom Scott director of surveillance of the casino. This time Sharon Powers provided the locations of where to look for her husband and the 95,000 square foot casino. We did a recreation and did a walkthrough on where if we were the suspect where we would have gone through certain areas and we pulled some tapes, eventually we were able to identify just from his shoes in a particular location where the suspect was standing.

We pulled a bunch of more shots, connected the shoes. We finally put some legs to the shoes and we're able to identify a person in a distance shot. Walking through the casino from the upstairs, looking down towards the suspect, we then connected more shots and follow the suspect down an escalator walking past the table where the victim was playing and follow the, uh, suspect out through our front door on videotape.

The video was compelling and confirm Gerald Lee powers was in the casino that night, but it didn't prove that he had abducted or murdered Shannon Sanderson,

hoping for physical evidence that would connect powers to the victim. Investigators searched behind a Tavern and Mississippi where power's wife claimed he had buried the victim's jewelry suspect had told her they were wrapped in tin for under a couch in the back.

Just as Mrs. Powers described investigators located a small bundle of foil inside. They found pink plastic wrap holding rings identified by the victim's husband is belonging to Shannon. Now they needed to prove forensically. The Gerald Lee powers had in fact, been the one who rapped them. Investigators went to power's home to search for the source of that plastic in the kitchen.

They found a roll of pink wrap.

They forwarded the roll along with the bundled rings to the lab for comparison.

while they waited for the results. Investigators turned their attention to the pink artificial nail found inside power's car. After he was arrested in

Texas.

Yeah, autopsy photos, uh, investigators found at least two nails were missing from the victim's hand. If the nail from the car matched those remaining on the victim's hand, it would prove that Shannon had been in power's car that night, but there was a problem Shannon had already been buried and her husband was against exhuming.

Her remains. She had already been entered. And so we had, uh, a hearing in court to have her uh disinterred and. Uh, to have the ability to examine these fingernails, to see if they were in fact, uh, her fingernails or not against her husband's wishes. The judge ordered the body exhumed in early July three months after the murder investigators retrieved the body of Shannon centers remaining artificial nails were removed and sent to the lab for comparison with the others.

the results were negative. The nail and the car wasn't heard.

investigators hope. The other evidence at the FBI lab in Washington, DC would provide more promising results inside the tinfoil ball recovered in Mississippi examiners. Remove the pink plastic wrap wound tightly around some rings. The FBI needed to connect the rings physically to Gerald Lee powers to do so.

Examiners compared the plastic, they were wrapped into the sample retrieved from power's home, the FBI agent who examined it indicated that it wasn't the exact piece that, uh, was, was torn off, but that it matched that role. Exactly. As far as the polymers and the dye and all that, which showed that this was the source that the, uh, the material had come from, that was wrapped around.

It was the first piece of forensic evidence linking powers to the victim. But the case was by no means complete more compelling proof came from a single fiber among several found in powers. Otherwise immaculate car. We have a dress fiber that was found in the vehicle that he was driving that night that matches the fiber from the dress that the victim was wearing.

Um, and that was very significant as well. Authorities were convinced that Gerald Lee powers had murdered Shannon Sanderson, but they weren't convinced he acted alone. They believed it was possible that others from her past could claim a motive for wanting Shannon dead. Memphis prosecutor, Jerry kitchen, decided to confirm it with powers himself.

So we went to Laredo to interview, uh, the defendant before we. Charged him with this murder. Uh, and there was the possibility if he cooperated and was able to prove to us that someone else was involved, that we were withdrawal seeking the death penalty. Uh, but there was nothing that he was able to provide us with.

So we were convinced then at that point that no one else had been involved in her, uh, abduction and murder and proceeded with charging him alone. How has had plenty of time to contemplate this murder. He watched her for several hours in the casino, then followed her for another hour back to Memphis. He had ample time to change his mind.

Instead, he hardened his resolve.

Get out of there, get ducted, a mother of three robbed her, then shot her at point blinding the criminal court in Tennessee. Didn't need much time to decide powers fate. After deliberating only 15 minutes. The jury recommended death for the murder of Shannon Sams, Gerald Lee powers awaits execution at Riverbend maximum security institution in Tennessee.

8 MURDER OF SARA TOKARS

In 1992, a young mother was done down in front of her children. Police searched for answers, but found nothing. Then family members offered a startling clue.

You'd be taking local and federal agents to untangle and intricate web of money, drugs, and order to capture the architects of a heartbreaking crime.

Two young boys were the only witnesses to their mother's murder. The horrible crime appeared unmotivated, senseless and random. I'm Jim former head of the FBI's New York office. The victim, the wife of a prominent Atlanta attorney was also a woman burdened with a secret. You FBI believe that secret led to her death.

They helped its discovery with also lead to her killer.

November 29th, 1992, Atlanta, Georgia

travelers returned home. Thanksgiving holiday, I'm ready to get nine-year-old Sarah tow cars under two children had spent the long weekend with her parents.

Well known lawyer and judge was away on business. After a nine hour drive, they arrived safely in their suburban Atlanta neighborhood of Marietta.

The house was dark as they pulled into the driveway.

but it was not empty.

Sarah did not see a man waiting in the shadows of the garage. He brandished a weapon. The gunman forced Sarah, back into the SUV.

The terrified woman had a six-year-old at her side and a four year old, still asleep in the car.

She had no choice.

the man put his gun to Sarah's head and told her to drive towards the city.

She followed instructions.

As they reached an empty development. He told her to turn off. She refused.

She pleaded with him to let her children go

answer with a single gunshot to her head. As the gunman grabbed her purse and flat vehicle kept rolling. The children's still inside.

When it came to a stop, Sarah six-year-old son had to reach across his mother's body to turn off the ignition

and buckled his groggy four year old brother from his car seat, then ran to the nearest house.

They're a neighbor called 911

officers responded to the report of a possible homicide in the vicinity of power's road.

Dispatch.

homicide. Detectives arrived as officers fanned out to search for the gunman.

Police briefed them on the spot. The two young boys who witnessed the shooting, identified the victim as their mother's Sarah Tokara,

their father, Fred tow cars was out of town. Police were already trying to contact him.

Forensic technicians examined the vehicle where it stopped. It might be trace evidence outside as well as inside the car. Right. And analysis confirmed with the boys and toward police. The gunman was sitting directly behind Sarah tow cars. When he pulled the trigger

blood spatter pattern suggested he had used a shotgun

detectives knew it would be difficult to get detailed information from children. So young. Especially after such a traumatic experience,

the oldest one is six years old would try his best

He said the killer was a black male wearing jeans, a sweatshirt, and a cap.

Could not be more specific. The boy didn't know which way the killer had run after he grabbed his mother's car. But he said the weapon looked like a Pirate's gun that you would see on TV.

Detectives were not sure what he meant. Maybe the autopsy would tell them.

detectives tracked down relatives, living in the area to take custody of the boys until their father. Could we located.

At least learned the family's address by running the plates on the vehicle.

They continued the investigation as a tow cars home where the abduction had occurred.

In the living room, they found a security dowel lying next to a sliding glass door. The killer had likely entered the house here. The home security system had not been activated. No alarm sounded was the intruder entered. Perhaps a burglar had taken advantage of the lack security and Sarah surprised in when she returned home, whoever the burglar was, he hadn't left any trace evidence at the tow cars home. There was little to go on according to Cobb County, chief, detective Arthur, old red. At this point, we just really didn't know what happened was this was a. In a upper middle class neighborhood. Uh, this was a, uh, uh, a mother with her two children.

And this of this type of crime was just, just didn't occur in this area at all. Uh, the most serious crime we had probably vandalism. Uh, so, uh, nationally, uh, we were really baffled as to what had happened and w and why.

Sarah's eldest son worked with a police sketch artist and described the men in the dark who had killed his mother, the drawing of a thin black man wearing a knit hat was released to the public.

But the six years its description was too vague to elicit any viable leads.

The victim's husband, Fred Tokara was contacted at his hotel in Montgomery, Alabama. He returned to Atlanta immediately.

As a criminal defense attorney, tow cars was aware he would be considered an early suspect in his way wife's murder. He had his own attorney present when he spoke to authorities

clear established his alibi. So police could pursue more promising lead

tech has confirmed that at the time of the murder. Pred tow cars was in Alabama. He had been visiting a client incarcerated in the Montgomery jail. Yeah.

The grieving husband assured police that he and Sarah had a strong marriage.

He would do anything he could to help find her killer.

All right guys, tow cars agreed to walk detectives through that.

As far as he knew the doors were locked and the security rod was in place when he left from Montgomery, um, claimed that they had intentionally left the alarm off because a plumber was scheduled to fix the hot water heater over the weekend.

We can talk ours lead detectives to the basement where he kept his home office. He said he usually had about $1,500 locked in the safe. Now it was open and empty. I did keep some cash in there. It's combination was hidden in a nearby file. Only he and his wife knew it was there. Perhaps Sarah had taken the money on her trip to Florida

is also possible that the burglar had found the combination and taking the cash. Ultimately Tokers couldn't specify how much money, if any was missing to police. Nothing else in the house seemed disturbed and no clues pointed to the killer's identity. A lot of people were frightened. A lot of people were just couldn't believe that this would happen to a mother in front of her children and especially in the neighborhood where it occurred.

So there was a lot of, uh, uh, a lot of pressure on the department to, to, to find who'd killed her.

Police hope the coroner's report would give them more lab examiners confirmed that Sarah togas had been killed with a four, 10 shotgun to a child. If that type of weapon had been sawed off, it might look like a 17th century flintlock pistol used by pirates on TV. And it's only the plastic wadding and buckshot were recovered from the SUV.

Because no shell casing had been ejected. They would not be able to match anything to a specific weapon. If one were later, maybe 14, the examiner discovered no foreign hairs, fibers, or fingerprints on the body.

Yeah. None of us killer had left. Nothing that could lead investigators to his identity.

or assistant United States, attorney, buddy Parker, like many members of the Atlanta community was stunned by the news of the murder. We had a discussion that morning about the notoriety of the homicide, it being the wife of Fred tow cars who was known, uh, within the legal community, uh, having been a former assistant district attorney for Fulton County.

Uh, I was familiar with, uh, Fred tow cars in his role as a criminal defense lawyer, in a matter that was didn't pending in our office. They matter regarding, um, the investigation of a particular drug,

Fred Dzhokhar's lucrative criminal defense practice brought him into contact with many men accused at federal drug charges. Rarely does such a murder have a simple motive solving the case would not be easy.

The following day two women came to the Cobb County police station. Sarah Tokara his sister and her cousin had a file. They needed to show detective

Sarah had entrusted her sister with the file three years earlier.

time. Sarah made her promise to take it to police if anything ever happened.

and what appeared to be lists of Fred tow cars banking. Accounts and their balances. How long have you known them suggested that the papers might be related to Sarah's attempt to divorce? Fred,

her sister's marriage was not as strong as Fred had led police to. I know what you've been doing. Sarah wanted a divorce, but whenever she broached the subject, he threatened to use his legal connections to get sole custody of their children. All right. Sorry guys. Let me tell you, Sarah was Travis ever hope to divorce Fred and keep her children?

She needed leverage after the incident, Sarah had secretly copied some of Fred's files and gave them to her sister for safekeeping.

She suspected they outlined illegal activities. He might be involved

if that were so they could be. Only leverage against him in court.

Investigators reviewed the files carefully.

Perhaps they would help police determine whether Sarah Tokara, his death was a botched robbery. Or a carefully planned conspiracy

Cobb County detectives called the FBI office in Atlanta for help. They hope that special agent Michael could determine a Fred Tokara. His bank statements was somehow linked to the murder. We were contacted by the Cobb County authorities, uh, concerning the documents they had discovered, which were brought to them.

By a cyber of tow cars, his sister and cousin, which revealed that Mr. Tokarevs or husband had been involved in setting up offshore bank accounts in offshore corporation,

it would take time for agent and his team to unravel the names and finances on those documents to see if they had something or nothing to do with the death of Sarah tow cars.

On December 3rd, 1997, four days after the shooting, Sarah Tokarevs was laid to rest.

Her two children were left. Mothers

investigators still had no leads that pointed to the identity of her killer. Whoever had killed the young mother was still out on the streets.

Just after Thanksgiving, 1997, the FBI and local investigators continued their search for the lone gunman who shot and killed Sarah tow cars. The wife of a prominent Atlanta attorney in front of her young children.

Six year old child had given a vague description of the suspect to police in Cobb County, Georgia, but they still had no solid leads.

Copies of her husband's bank statements was sent to the FBI field office in Atlanta for closer scrutiny.

Special agent Michael hope to provide insight as to whether the documents might somehow be connected to Sarah Tokarevs murder.

Once we reviewed these documents, it revealed that Mr. Tokara. Set up offshore banks and corporations, not only in the Turks and Caicos, but in Montserrat and in The Bahamas, uh, Lee, these documents also showed that he had set up numerous corporations and nominees names in Atlanta, Georgia area. Nominees are people who in name only had dummy corporations for purposes of money laundering.

Although Fred tow cars had never been accused of money laundering himself. He was an expert on the subject, buddy Parker, a former assistant us attorney was aware that tow cars was not only a well-known lawyer. He was also a certified public accountant. Fred tow cars was known within the Atlanta legal community as, uh, a person who held himself out to be an expert in, uh money-laundering.

Uh, and in fact, conducted, uh, lectures for law enforcement authorities, uh, at the state level, uh, on money laundering. Investigating the finances of a man like Fred tow cars would be a delicate business. He was well liked and well connected among Atlanta's power, right.

Was well known in Cobb County. He was also well-known in, uh, political circles. And as much as he had been appointed as a assistant municipal court judge, and he had been an assistant solicitor for Fulton

County. He had, uh, uh, a lot of friends in high political places and helped on numerous campaigns, uh, of, uh, state and local, uh, officials.

I'm wondering if you have any investigators again, met with tow cars and his attorney.

They told him they believed his business dealings could be connected to his wife's killing and asked him about his clients. And your wife mentioned anything to you. Fred tow cars admitted several were violent drug dealers who operated in dangerous

particular was reputed to have been a major cocaine supplier in the Atlanta area.

The dealer had returned home to Detroit after another one of tow cars, clients had allegedly forced him out of the South.

not long after he was done down in front of his mother's home. The murder weapon, a handgun found later in the nearby alley. Had been traced back to a gun shop North of Atlanta,

Tokara suggested that the dealers remaining crew, or even those who murdered him could have had Sarah killed to send a message to the lawyer. We can arrange that taken to the detective, secured a warrant to search the attorney's office, to see if they could find any link to the killer in his papers.

that night, local investigators and IRS agents conducted a thorough search of the office. They confiscated files, date books, and business calendars dating back several years, but found no direct clues to the murder.

In the margins of Tokara datebooks agents did find notations of offshore accounts.

Total deposited in these accounts far exceeded the amount Tokara claimed on his taxes either. Yeah.

It looked as if Fred tow cars and used his expertise in money laundering to his own financial advantage.

and federal officials met with representatives of the Atlanta United States attorney's office. So that's a good start dress. I suspected Fred Tokers illegal activities went far beyond money laundering Browns while ownings money-laundering was already on our radar screen. If you will. Secondly, now we have evidence coming out of the tow cars home of all short bank accounts with those two.

Clear facts. Uh, we felt that there was a firm basis to open an investigation formally on Fred tow cars. Dick Parker learned that in August of 1992, the DEA had arrested one of Tokara his clients in a sting operation. His name was Anthony Brown. Brown had a reputation as a cocaine dealer in Atlanta. The day before agents had intercepted one of his couriers in Texas and seized more than 100 kilos of cocaine.

Inside the trunk of Brown's car agents found $50,000 a year.

They also found documents. Revealing Fred tow cars was more than Brown's defense attorney. He had incorporated and Atlanta nightclub for the drug dealer. It was believed by law enforcement, that the nightclub was a front to help launder the drug proceeds of the drug trafficking organization. That Brown was a member of.

DEA agent Jeff Dolman had participated in the sting operation to arrest Brown Parker. Hope Darwin's drug trafficking case would help with the murder investigation. What had happened as a result of a homicide of Mrs. Tow cars was that the light got turned on fed tow cars, his pass of what, what he had been doing for the past several years in what was illuminated.

Was that he'd been involved with several drug traffickers in the Atlanta area.

Investigators wondered how deep that involvement went. Police re-interviewed Tokara neighbors to see if they had missed anything. I was wondering if on Sunday, one close friend confirmed that Sarah wanted to divorce her husband, but she was afraid of him.

Not long before she was murdered. Sarah confided that she had found some of her husband's documents that seemed suspicious. According to the neighbor, Sarah said these weren't simply lists of offshore accounts. They were stronger proof of criminal activities. Listen, I have to give you a call back about a week and a half before Sarah tow cars is a murder.

Uh, So they were tow cars, uh, explained to her, uh, that she now had the goods on Fred, that she had found documents or records that indicated he had engaged in or was engaging in tax evasion. And that she, uh, she was going to go to the authorities with this information and she could then get a divorce. If Sarah had confronted her husband with the evidence, it might've motivated him to harm her

investigators. Additionally found the name of a Tokara private investigator.

PEI admitted to agents that tow cars had hired him to approach drug dealers about laundering their profits. He was listed as one of the owners, along with Fred tow cars of another Atlanta nightclub, according to special agent Michael twice, we determined that he was an owner of a company. But through our further investigation, we realized that he was a nominee.

And when I say the word nominee, I mean, the fact that he was delegated to the person being legally responsible as it being an owner of the club. But he, in actuality, he was, it's not Fred Tokas who constructed the entire scheme. According to the private eye, tow cars, ported reputed drug dealers, like Anthony Brown, men who had a lot of cash, but no place to invest it without raising suspicions of the IRS tow cards, a money laundering expert.

Proposed depositing their drug profits in offshore accounts and in businesses like clubs that operated primarily on a cash basis, the money could then be filtered through legitimate financial institutions

with launder. The money is even though it's still in cash, you would pay entertainers. On the paper, $15,000. When they actually, now that you paid him $5,000 cash Tokers would receive thousands for each transaction. He was actively involved knowing that these people were drug traffickers. And what they were doing with their money.

The object was to open corporations, mainly nightclubs cash businesses, where they could easily hide their assets, where they could easily run their drug proceeds through them. It's already believed the connection between Fred tow cars and drug traffickers had somehow led to his wife's murder.

But the details were elusive. You're back in our car. Now, weeks after the murder of Sarah tow cars, a man capable of murdering an innocent mother in front of her children remanded large.

Got a shotgun blast in the back of that number 1992, several weeks after Sarah Tokarevs was killed, federal and state authorities had still not found the lone gunman and still had no clues to his identity

shortly before she was brutally murdered. Sarah believes she had discovered papers in her husband's law office that documented his illegal activities.

Former us prosecutor, buddy Parker believed that Sarah had likely threatened to expose Fred tow cars with those documents, unless he agreed to a divorce that began to give us a feeling that, uh, say we're tow cars was murdered to keep her mouth shut about her knowledge or her belief about her husband's role and involvement in laundering, drug money for drug traffickers.

Fred Toker is not only represented violent drug dealers. He had gone into business with them. Sure. Investigators now had evidence Tokers clients were laundering money through several nights.

his wife had threatened to expose him tow cars, as well as his clients had a lot to lose.

The FBI took a hard look at the nightclubs. The attorney had incorporated special agent Michael had to Wade through piles of state records, searching for a name that could link tow cars directly to the murder. We started reviewing a company, incorporation records and a liquor license and business license that, uh, Mr.

Tow cars had incorporated. We started looking at these different clubs to see actually who owned them major drug suppliers, like Al Brown contributed the funds, a middleman, purchased the clubs and took our setup. The entire deal as DEA agent Jeff dome. Discovering, they didn't really trust. Mr. Tokara is the laundry money in offshore bank accounts.

It's too elaborate. They wanted their money where they could touch it, where they could feel it, where they could use it every day, where they could buy cars with it in. So the laundering, in essence, in this investigation turned towards the laundering of money through nightclubs, through incorporation. Oh, the nightclubs AI agents interviewed employees of the nightclubs over time.

They were able to piece together the structure of the business, its owners and its the conference to attorney Parker. It was like assembling a complex puzzle.

the picture of how, uh, the nightclub money-laundering was structured was really developed through insiders through inside drug traffickers, who ultimately decided to cut plea agreements with us and to cooperate and provide evidence. But nothing from the nightclubs pointed to Sarah took ours killer.

After months of frustration, Cobb County police finally got a break, a detective working on the case, got a tip from his brother, the deputy in nearby Fulton County. The deputy remembered seeing Fred tow car's name in the file for a businessman who had an outstanding, a restaurant.

The businessman's name was Eddie Lawrence wanted for writing bad checks on one of tow cars, accounts of all tow cars, business associates, and clients. Eddie Lawrence was a name he had never mentioned to police it's already as quickly learned that Eddie Lawrence and Fred tow cars were involved in several cases.

This is together included construction, renovation, and mortgage companies. Tow cars had also defended Lawrence and several minor brushes with the law.

It was a long shot. But it was the only lead they had left.

Eddie Lawrence had drew Fred tow. Car's been granted access to some of the, uh, some of the, uh, most prominent individuals within the city. Uh, Fred would take Eddie to some of the big political fundraising functions. And all of a sudden Eddie was like I said, he's very presentable. He w he could certainly, uh, mingle and, and, and, uh, not being embarrassed at cocktail functions and things, and engage in conversations.

And, and so, uh, he, he was living this wonderful life and the way he got there was through Fred tow cars a few days later. The young businessman agreed to questioning after police discovered records of calls between he and tow cars. On the day of the murder. Eddie Lawrence said he had been in business with Fred tow cars for almost there've been inflamed.

The phone calls were all job-related. I knew nothing about Sarah Tokarevs murder. The detectives had Lawrence arrested on the bad check charge, and then released him on bond.

They wanted to see which one of tow cars, associates got nervous when they heard Lawrence was being investigated. This was a shock to me. When I heard about her death,

the plan worked.

The confidential informant contacted police.

the word on the street was that Eddie Lawrence had been looking for a Hitman prior to Sarah. Tokara his murder.

Pressured one of his employees to help him find someone to kill a woman who he claimed stood in the way of a lot of money

employee gave Lawrence a name. Curtis rower rower was a drug addict with a long rap sheet, including armed.

He needed money. Maybe he'd be interested,

although the informant didn't mention Fred Tokers by name investigators finally had a potential link between the victim's husband, Eddie Lawrence, and a Hitman

detectives interviewed Eddie Lawrence.

They questioned him about his relationship with tow cars.

He claimed no involvement in the murder. Police felt he was lying. We have a warrant you need on December 16th, 1992, police detained Lawrence and revoked his bail because of the flight.

They wanted him in custody when they went after Curtis rower.

the detectives immediately secured search and arrest warrants for a house in college park where rower was staying.

They proceeded with caution. If rower was capable of killing an innocent woman in cold blood, there was no telling what he might do when cornered.

December 22nd, 1992, three weeks. After a mother of two was murdered Cobb County police circled a home in college park to arrest suspected Hitman Curtis rower.

the woman who answered the door said she wasn't sure if rower was home,

an initial sweep of the house produced nothing. Still, they kept up their guard. One officer's thought he heard movement in a bedroom.

It was Curtis rower stay on the ground. He was unarmed. Lay down all the way down, bring your hands out. He spread rower was booked and charged with murder

that Eddie Lawrence, Fred Tokara, his business partner had offered him $5,000 to kill Sarah tow cars. But rower was too scared to go through with it. He said Lawrence was the one who had caused Sarah's death.

Rower admitted that he had carjacked the family, but when Sarah Tokers stopped, he said that he couldn't pull the trigger at that moment. Eddie Lawrence ran up to the car, screaming for Roy or just shoot Lawrence, grabbed the shotgun and it went off. Killing Sarah Tokara

both men then fled in March's car.

they'll police believe rower cwas downplaying his role. Sarah's six year old son was the only other witness they had to refute his claim.

He remembered only one shooter. The boy would be forced to identify the man who terrorized his family from a lineup unless Eddie Lawrence corroborated rower's story

authorities charged Eddie Lawrence with conspiracy to commit murder, but Lawrence refused to confirm or deny rower's statement.

Hello County police notified Fred Tokers that Eddie Lawrence and Curtis rower had been formally charged with his wife's murder. He received the news at Sarah's parents house in Florida, where he was vacationing with his sons for the holiday don't have phones. So the police, they arrested someone. Thank God for that.

His relatives later said that while the rest of the family expressed relief, Fred Tokers did not.

He seemed despondent.

The arrest of Lawrence rower had made national headlines. Tow cars was caught in that same spotlight and refuse to give any statements to the press.

Because of the suspected Hitman story conflicted with Tokara son's version. The six year old was asked to view a suspect lineup. Police explained that though he would be able to see five men staring at him. They would not be able to see him. The one way mirror would prevent that the child said he was ready.

Investigators called for the men.

All of them resembled the boy's description of his mother's killer.

the detectives reassured him that he could take as much time as he needed

it was no use. The child was either too young or too frightened to remember the killer's face.

When relatives tried to reach Fred tow cars in Florida to inform him he was nowhere to be found,

left the company of his in-laws and returned to his, his hotel room, uh, where, uh, no one heard from him. And the following morning, they tried to, uh, raise him on the telephone. They tried to find him and there were no responses.

Consent Sarah's father rushed to the hotel where tow cars, Mustang, bread, bread, bread.

Fred tow cars had swallow the handful of sleeping pills, and we washed it down with beer.

The manager of the hotel quickly called an ambulance. He had apparently attempted to take his life after hearing that at Eddie Lawrence, uh, uh, this, this, uh, business partner of his, uh, had been arrested for the murder of his, of his wife.

Sarah's father found a note written in Fred Tokarevs handwriting on the table, beside the bed

in the locked hotel room. Fred Tokarevs wrote a long rambling note apologizing for the pain and suffering his lifestyle had inflicted upon his family. He wrote that Sarah was a great woman.

Then on the day before Christmas Eve, Fred Tokara swallowed a handful of sleeping pills

enough to kill him.

Fred Tokarevs lay on the bed, barely breathing. If he died, the truth about his wife's murder might die with him. Come on bread. Yes. Yes. There's been an emergency late December of 1992. Fred tow cars, the ones prominent Atlanta attorney now suspected in his wife's murder, lay motionless in a Florida hotel room from an overdose of sleeping

he was rushed to a nearby hospital where they were able to revive him. Um, thank you for coming down today. After his release, he held a press conference, tough time for myself and also for my children. He told the public that he was very depressed and that media was not making it easy. It was terrible.

Tokers had gone to the extent of establishing residency in Florida to avoid the attention. Way through this. So did he believe that justice would soon be served?

The FBI believed justice would soon be served as well. Convince the tread tow cars had used his business, associate Eddie Lawrence to hire a Hitman to kill Fred's wife. Sarah, the team of federal and local investigators would use federal racketeering statutes known as Rico to prosecute cars.

I think a Rico case to prove Sarah has had been killed to protect her husband's illegal activities meant outlining those activities in detail. The Rico statute, it attacks basically this conspiracy of individuals who are out committing all types of different crimes, not necessarily together, but they're all for the benefit of this, of this criminal group.

To exist to continue to exist and to make money. Like thanks for coming together a little bit. I appreciate all the federal grand jury named Tokarevs is an unindicted co-conspirator in the homicide though. Tow car's partner, Eddie Lawrence had remained silent after seven months in prison. Investigators hope the public indictment might encourage Lawrence to testify against tow cars.

Not long after the Atlanta us attorney's office received a phone call that Eddie Lawrence was ready to cooperate in exchange for sentencing consideration. You got some work to do.

For Lawrence, his long awaited statement, investigators secured a remote location in Georgia. That would be monitored by chopper surveillance. The agent Jeff Dolman was part of the team that needed to make sure nothing

We were there before Mr. Lawrence was brought in, uh, his location had been, kept a secret from everybody involved. Uh, the only people that knew of where Mr. Lawrence was actually being held at that time were the cab County police department. Mr. Lawrence at that time was a key witness. In this investigation and his safety was paramount to everyone

inside a fortified house. Eddie Lawrence told investigators that he in tow cars were not just partners in the construction business. They were also involved in laundering drug money.

Lawrence told FBI special agent Michael the details of the scheme. Okay, Mr. Tow cars more in hand to try to solicit drug clients and the various night clubs and bring them to him so he could launder their money. And in turn also set up Eddie Lawrence into several businesses. Yeah, we can get this one just a little bit.

They remember Lawrence owed his success to tow cars. He also the attorney $70,000 in business stats, Fred tow cars approached Eddie Lawrence indicating that, you know, that say right now was going to try to divorce him and take everything he had. And he wasn't going to let that happen. And he couldn't afford to allow her to do that to him.

And he wanted her to kill. Lawrence refused initially, although he had been involved in drug dealing, he had never been involved in murder. Mr. Lawrence said, we'll just let her have the house and the kids in the cars. And Mr. Tow car said, I had worked so hard. I'm not going to let her have it. Lauren said that Tokara has planned the murder for several months.

His first idea was to have Sarah shot in his office, but decided the couple's home was a better location to take their money. Took ours, was to pay Lawrence twenty-five thousand dollars for the hit. Mr. Lawrence advised that Mr. Tow cars wanted to be out of town and that. For Mr. Lawrence to commit the murder, uh, as a burglary, it basically, uh, in front of his children, uh, which is very unusual.

He told Mr. Lawrence that the kids would get over it, that they're young and it wouldn't bother them saying that their mother, it was murdered. I found that Lawrence admitted he didn't have the nerve to kill an innocent woman. So he hired Curtis roar.

after rowers shut. Sarah Tokers Lawrence drove him away from the scene.

since he cooperated Lawrence earned 12 and a half years, for his part in setting up the murder. The Hitman he hired. Curtis rower was sentenced to life without parole.

For the time being tow cars was still a free man.

Cars had custody of his two children are concerned. Um, during this time and the arrest of Mr. was there could be some harm done to the children. And Mr. was, uh, was aware that he'd been. Watch the media was still down in Florida. At the time, he knew that people were watching them daily and we had to develop a plan to get Mr.

Tow cars out of the house where there'd be no harm done to the children or to himself, and try to affect the arrest.

The agents knew tow cars hated the press. They posed as reporters lurking around the condo, hoping to elicit a response from the wanted man. The game plan at that time was to have Mr. Tokara has come out and check us out, which he had done previously to other people that had been parked in the area.

The plan worked well. Okay. He came downstairs, he called the police.

Local officers arrived aware of the rules.

Fred tow cars emerged from his condo to file a complaint.

Instead he was arrested. Fred Tokara pleaded not guilty to the charges against him. But separate state and federal juries found him guilty of racketeering money-laundering murder for hire and murder. He was sentenced to four life terms with no chance of we're rolling for elevating his greed beyond the life of his wife and children.

He will never be free again.

ABOUT THE AUTHOR

Rachel writes the strange, unique, and often wacky side of criminality.

Humans have a strange and lasting fascination with the dark and macabre. We're hooked on stories about crime and murder.